HOW TO GET WHAT YOU WANT FROM ANYONE

Understanding The Secret Of Analyzing Anyone

TESSA DAVID

The information herein is provided for educational purpose exclusively, and is universal. The presentation of the information is without contractual agreement or any kind of warranty assurance.

All trademarks and brands within this book are for clarifying purposes only and are owned by the owners themselves, not affiliated with this document.

Disclaimer

All erudition supplied in this book are specified for educational purpose only. The author is not in any way accountable for any results that emerges from utilizing this book. Constructive efforts have been made to render information that is both precise and effective, however the author is not to be held responsible for the accuracy or use/misuse of this information.

CONTENT

INTRODUCTION

How to manipulate and doing mind manipulation is a skill that is innate to each of us. Everybody is born with it. Each individual reacts and interacts to one another. That is how manipulation works in the society. It brings people in and out. It is the way we communicate with one another.

How to manipulate is as important as how to communicate and relate to people. When we relate and convey our thoughts to our peers we lure them to listen to us and understand our own beliefs if not agree to it. We base our success on how people respond to the kind of thinking that we have. If we get favorable responses from people, we will feel satisfied and that satisfaction builds up our whole being. If we somehow fail to be understood we often resort to arguments because our subconscious fights for the manipulative tactics of others. We simply do not want to be manipulated but somehow we tend to forget that every decision and actions that we take are only products of mind manipulation by others.

The saddest part is that we often fail to realize that we need to manipulate in order to survive and to be successful. If we only aim for survival we don't need to practice a lot of mind manipulation techniques. But should we settle down for less? We want to become more than and larger than ourselves.

First thing we need to consider is that we need to understand that manipulation is not negative. Somehow, negative connotations impact the way we deal with people. We thought, being frank and direct about telling others our need is a kind of manipulation and therefore is bad. We thought that when we ask someone to do the things our way is a kind of manipulation then we refrain from trying to ask for help. We just then fail to realize that we miss the chance that could have been a new door for an opportunity.

We take pride too much for ourselves about doing playing fair while the world is not. What we are trying to achieve though is not to trick everyone and mean them bad. We just like to open our eyes on the opportunities that just awaiting to be unlocked. If we put up a cocktail party because we want to invite and be acquainted with somebody who we know can help us well with our interest is a kind of technique that we need.

Mind manipulation is within us. We do not need special psychic power to be able to manipulate people and be successful. We just need to know the techniques and skillfully practice it.

We all do it

Do you ever take some one for granted? They will do what you want - so no worries. You may feel okay about this but there may be signs of discontent from the other person - whether this is your spouse or child at home or colleague or subordinate at work. You suspect they may not be quite as happy and friendly as you would like to believe. One possible reason for this state of affairs might be that, without being conscious of this, you have a tendency to manipulate them into doing or thinking what you want: getting them to comply with your desires. There need be no bad intent but nevertheless others can notice in our behaviour what we ourselves are blind to.

Effects when we manipulate others

There are recognisable effects if this is happening. The other person might express doubts about what to think. They might feel distressed if they don't happen to act in accordance with your wishes. Or perhaps they might feel they have little choice but to follow your lead. In extreme cases the cumulative effect of manipulation is for the victim to feel a sense of powerlessness.

Many of these signs were present in the example of Peter and Nina Hemming. The manipulative behaviour in this case gives something of the flavour of what happens when one partner unreasonably wants to get his own way regardless of the other's preferences. Peter kept promising Nina they would marry. She bought a dress, told her friends, made excited plans. He even booked a venue - using her mother's money. But three times he called the wedding off.

When their children were baptised, he refused to attend the family gathering. When she got a job at a Mercedes dealership, he said "I'll pay you to stay at home." He also refused to allow Nina's eldest daughter by a previous relationship to see her father. He got her to allow him access to her mail which he scrutinised together with her bank statements. The effect of all Peter's manipulation and unreasonable behaviour was that Nina left him.

What it means to manipulate someone

It is part of normal life to trade and exchange favours. And so in most relationships both partners may try to influence the other to some extent. This doesn't necessarily mean manipulation. To actually manipulate the other person, one uses underhand and insidious pressure often of a subtle nature. This seems to come naturally to many of us even when young.

No one act of manipulation of itself can be seen as bad. I would say that it is only when one considers the pattern of behaviour that one realizes what is really going on.

Some people can recognise their desire to manipulate others and try to stop.

Ways we use to manipulate others

To avoid the tendency to manipulate someone you may want to watch out in case you are conducting yourself in one or more of the following ways:

Unfairly expecting something of the other person and constantly expressing what to them is an unreasonable demand. It might be for example asking a worker that he or she work unpaid overtime.

Implying threats for example of showing a spouse up in front of others

Being judgmental by unfairly accusing the other person of having, for example, a selfish or uncaring attitude.

Putting the other person down. This can be very subtle such as a fierce look or glance, unpleasant tone of voice, rhetorical comments, or subtle sarcasm.

Deceiving the other person by making false claims for example that an insult was only a joke.

Punishing their behaviour you don't want by nagging, crying, giving 'the silent treatment', making explosive angry outbursts or yelling to get compliance.

Some of these points are discussed further by Harriet Braiker, in her book Who's Pulling Your Strings? How to Break The Cycle of Manipulation.

Self-orientation as a cause of manipulation

Do most of us really try to manipulate other people to get our own way? Even just from time to time and not being obvious about it? One consideration is the theory that we each have a natural tendency towards self-orientation. An inclination that can result in selfishness.

Just as well you might say, for how else can we survive in this competitive world? However, the usual spiritual perspective is to bear in mind the needs of others: not prioritising self but balancing one's own wants with those of others. Perhaps we might ask ourselves this question. Is there a danger in making self-orientation the chief of our motives. In other words having a self-concern that is over and above consideration for the rights of others?

It seems to follow that when self-orientation rules then we always want to get our own way, to win the argument and be seen to be in the right, to feel superior to others and dominate them. Is such an attitude not shown by wanting to manipulate someone so we gain control for the sake of self-interest?

The bad news is that being manipulative can only result in poor personal relationships. This means we would miss out on the chance of a union of mutual respect and care.

The following chapters will discuss the importance of learning the way to analyze people and learning the way to control your visual communication when around people. You'll be conversant in an instance where someone is saying something to you, but their visual communication communicates a completely different thing to you. So, what does one believe? The spoken words or body language? Consistent with global research, the reality always lies within the manner of its delivery. Note that this is often to not say that words don't matter; they are doing matter tons. But, if the words and therefore the mode of delivery don't match, people are sure to believe what they observe as against what they hear. Though spoken words convey information like data and facts, visual communication reveals deeper information like your intentions, attitude, and your general state of being. Though people tell lies to save lots of the people they love from getting hurt or protect their interests, never be surprised when your visual communication gives you away. This is often because the visual communication communicates differently from what you really say. As such, it's easy to inform what an individual really feels a few situation or conversation by studying their visual communication. This book seeks to show you ways to research people and use the knowledge you get ethically for your own benefit or for his or her benefit also.

Being conscious of what your body communicates or what people communicate with their body is vital at ensuring that you simply retain the facility or control of a situation that would potentially cause negative effects if not handled professionally. Moreover, it's common for people to interact in sales deals or negotiations at some point in life. Within the following chapters, you'll learn the perfect visual communication to exude when engaging in sales deals also as negotiations. Practicing particular postures, gestures, and expressions help in creating the knowledge and message you would like to convey more clearly, and it also gets people to believe your words. On the opposite hand, by understanding people, observing and interpreting their visual communication and actions ensures that you simply have the whip hand when responding to their behavior and getting them to accept as true with what you'll be communicating. Therefore, if you would like to reinforce your interpersonal communication and learn what other people's visual communication communicates, control their signs and signals, this book are going to be of much help. The more conscious an individual is of the unspoken words, the more they're ready to understand what people really mean and communicate in actual sense. Learning how the visual communication communicates and to perfectly interpret that takes commitment and far dedication.

Throughout the subsequent chapters, you'll learn the meanings behind the various movements, gestures, facial expressions, and postures that folks display in several instances. You'll understand the way to clarify your message, decipher lies, and demonstrate good behavior by understanding people. You furthermore may find out how to camouflage once you don't wish to be discovered, especially when lying to guard the people you're keen on.

In order to form this book as beneficial because it should be to you, the content has been structured consistent with different topics and scenarios. This ensures that it easy for you to flip at will to the section you deem more relevant to your situation or flip to the section that holds the knowledge you would like to find out. Every chapter identifies the detailed information and action an individual should deem effective behavior. Therefore, if you would like to enhance your ability to read other people's actions and inner feelings also as intentions, this is often the proper investment which will offer you all the answers that you simply cannot find readily on the web.

In addition, it pays to be in your right state that matches what you say. Staying proud and sure about your words and actions indicates that you simply are authentic. This makes it easier for people to believe your words and provides you the facility to be the simplest you'll be. As an example, it's beneficial for sales and marketing executives to master the art of visual communication that they will apply when trying to hit an affect clients who need much convincing. This ensures that the clients read exactly what they assert from their visual communication and gauge them as trustworthy. For instance, hanging on the sidelines, having a frowned face, and head burrowed on the chest means you're watching something or someone suspiciously. On the opposite hand, applying animated expressions and gestures when working with a gaggle of individuals implies that you simply are conscious of what you're saying and ready for subsequent explanation for action.

It is important for people to know that the small things mean tons, and that they are often the difference between getting your dream job or deal. This is often because not even your intentions and thoughts are resistant to how the body reflects them in your facial expressions and movements. As an example, your boss may suggest something during your review interview that sounds stupid, and without your control, the eyes may roll, which can be deemed to be rude because you're required to be at your best behavior when addressing your boss. Fortunately, it's possible to make the state you desire to portray. This book seeks to show you ways to realize this during a bid to make sure that you simply are on the proper page with everyone you relate to or work with. You are doing not always need to experience the emotions that accompany the psychological state that you simply wish to project. As an example, it's possible to convey certainty when feeling doubtful about something. It all depends on how you control your body language; the inner world isn't one with the surface world. Therefore, it's possible to possess one thought within the inner world and convey a completely different thing within the outer world. That's what the important power of concerning people should be like. Indulge below to find out this and more.

There are many books on this subject on the market, thanks again for selecting this one! Every effort was made to make sure it's filled with the maximum amount useful information as possible, and please enjoy!

CHAPTER 1

TYPES OF PEOPLE BEHAVIOR

According to psychologists, the overall attitude of individuals greatly signifies their personality type. There are difference preference points of dichotomies which tend to represent different personality level during a person. These functions dimensions are usually dominant over the perceptions of the opposite liable for judging and perceiving relationships to influence the personality. Foremost, there's extraversion-introversion criterion, which signifies the direction of a person's energy liable for their expression. The energy during this concept focuses on the external world instead of the interior existence for the extroversion. On the opposite hand, introversion doesn't specialize in the external world.

The second criterion is that the sensing-intuition, which mainly focuses on the tactic through which an individual perceives a bit of data. Sensing perspective believes within the information from the surface world, while intuition believes within the information from within, which is out of imagination to be correct and viable to be considered. Thinking-feeling is another criterion for engaging personality type. The essential concept for thinking and feelings is to measure how an individual processes the incoming and existing information. On the thinking perspective, one makes a choice supported the thoughts analyzed logically by the mind.

On the opposite hand, feelings mean sort of a rule where one makes a choice supported emotions — how one tends to feel about something triggered the choice making process. Ultimately, there's a judging-perceiving criterion for identifying the personality trait of an individual. This criterion mainly concerns how one process already captures information to form contextual decisions, how the knowledge implementation takes the higher a part of this process. By judging, one has got to organize all the life events, the principles and plans to capture the larger concept of the knowledge. Perceiving means one has got to improvise the already existing information to explore alternatives. Here, one looks at the simplest perspective of the knowledge which inserts things or event at hand and the way to pursue it well to succeed in a sensible conclusion of the matter.

The four dichotomies offer all the possible permutations to yield the 16 combinations of various personality types. The likelihood of an individual having quite two personalities is extremely high, considering the dichotomies personality criterion. Therefore, with all this data, one can identify and interpret different personality types that exist within the world today. In any way possible, the personality of an individual is that the determinant of their success or failure in life, thus scrutinizing this basic knowledge enable one to urge full concept on the way to affect different personality. Besides, there's a likelihood of developing a productive relationship with these people supported the knowledge of how they operate, view things, and react towards different life challenges. The very fact that there are different personalities makes it possible for people to intermingle to make an excellent team.

Extroversion

Extroversion are often depicted as a top quality of being outgoing, caring, and getting to other people's feelings. Most of the time, the extroversion people become the middle of attention when out with people.

This personality type is believed to be one among the core traits related to sociability, assertiveness, talkativeness, and excitability.

Excitedly, these people always seek a chance for social stimulation to interact with others.

They're described as filled with life, energy, and positivity wherever they are going. In most cases, they're always seen because the ring leaders everywhere they're thanks to their assertiveness nature which tend to draw in more people towards them. Moreover, they're always out of their thanks to help others in completing a number of the activities. Who are going to be ready to avoid such people in their life, that one one that is usually there for you when in need, when there's a drag to be solved, and in any life-threatening situation which will mean much to others? The habit of extraversion of talking often makes them lively and adorable to be around them whenever. They're likely to form every boring situation livelier, thus taking control of all the circumstances which will be hazardous to people. Besides, they are doing not fear to require a risk which makes them much distinct in any setting. Their engagement in talkative behavior enables them to urge more energy and feel socially stimulated over the opposite behavioral traits. They get excited when new ideas are brought forth for discussion, which makes them play an excellent role in actualizing the new ideas and making it successful.

There are many speculations on the causes of extroversion behavior on people. The talk on the rationale why some people are extroverted while others aren't has been of much concern to several within the society. Consistent with psychologists, the key attributes of this behavior have always pegged to either nature or nurture. Many of us argue that these people have a robust genetic component, which is formed from 40 and 60 percent variance between introverts and extroversion behavioral attribution. Similarly, others argue that the trait could also be attributed to the variability of the trait linked to the difference in cortical arousal. It's been found that extroverts usually seek external stimulation, which arouses their cortical, which is liable for their explosive behavior. In comparison to introverts, they're much lively and sociable. They just like the company of others as compared to introverts who dread the corporate of the many people.

On the opposite hand, extroversion also attributed to the environmental impact on behavior. This is often where nature plays an enormous role in their character, where they'll have gained the trait from the sibling's character or the social associates in society. The shared experience plays a much bigger role during this part where the person is probably going to realize the behavior through acquisition from the people he or she mingles within the environment.

One may ask how extroversion impact our behavior, the influence it's on how we do things and react to different situations. Consistent with researchers, it's been found that the trait has much to try to with the tendency of our personality and career life we take. Most of the extroversion trait is related to a leadership role in every place they're or where there's a congregation of individuals. The high character put them one step before others. Extroverts have the habit of asserting themselves in groups, which makes them much likely to urge higher positions of influencing and controlling people ethically, which is far likely to profit everyone involved. Besides, they're less likely to experience anxiety over rejection or feedback, unlike their introvert counterparts.

In most cases, these people are highly recommended for jobs that need social interaction and much of independent work where they will engage their energy fully. They can't exercise their full potential for jobs like writing, programming, and engineering, which only appeal to people low in extroversion. Though research has revealed that this trait is a smaller amount common love it is perceived by many of us since there has been a likelihood of confusing it with other traits. Unfortunately, extroversion trait is considered overexcited and socially illiterate, making them attract the eye of individuals with an eq uivalent trait.

Neuroticism

These are people that are susceptible to mood disorder, self-consciousness, loneliness, and hypochondria q uite behavior. It's claimed to be one among big personality towards anxiety and depression, which usually exist as a results of negative feelings arising from within the person. Actually, these people aren't fun to be around thanks to such lonely behavior they possess. Consistent with research, neuroticism is seemed to predict the students' success in life. Moreover, it determines the motive behind the determination towards achieving great heights in life. The productivity of scholars generally lowered by the negativity inclined towards work and therefore the extent at which one exerts interest on what they are doing, how they are doing it, and therefore the general outcome of the work.

In times, neuroticism tends to supply an evolutionary advantage by listening to most of the negative outcomes of an occasion, which helps humans to survive in such events. Nevertheless, one will tend to settle on to lough upon an unsightly situation than run away. In most cases, neuroticism individuals always battle with maladaptive thoughts in their day to day activities, which makes them susceptive to depressions or anxiety when faced with different problems. Have you ever wondered why some people are likely to be threatened by negative events than others, why they have a tendency to be subjected to low self-esteem, which can impact their lives negatively? These are just ordinary people, and therefore the problem is that they need a weird personality that doesn't rhyme well with others. The extent of hysteria tends to heighten whenever they encounter unfamiliar events or once they get into a weird living situation, which stretches their imagination beyond the traditional conceptual grasp of that event.

The neuroticism trait has been related to people that are emotionally unstable and lack self- resilience with one among the smallest amount in society. Fortunately, a high scorer with this type of trait tends to be more impulsive and also are known for his or her tendency of worrying tons incorporated with short tempter when slightly revoked. They need relationship problems whereby they destroy a stable relationship out of their insecure and unstable emotional control. Besides, they're not emotionally intelligent, making their life encounter to be boring, filled with chaos, and conflict of interest, which normally crowd their judgment. They need trust issues whenever where they claim that somebody is using them or duped them on a particular deal. Raggedly they can't lack what to complain about, what to curse or accuse once they fail on a task. Getting alongside these people usually tends to be difficult thanks to this unattractive trait, which makes them lose on the special life gift of enjoyment. From the emotional perspective, it's derived that these people are more sensitive to threats and punishment, which can be poised on them. Deducting from the emotional perspective, one may tend to ask on their cognitive side. Studies put underway to look at on the cognitive side of the neuroticism people reveal that they need a chaotic, noisier mental system.

The chronic worrying related to neuroticism instills fear of being unwanted by people, and therefore the need for reassurance cloud their thinking. They always feel that they are doing not slot in a situation, belittling feeling, which makes them inferior and unfit for the task in hand. In most cases, they wonder if they need done anything wrong to offend anyone to deserve some treatment even once they aren't treated right as they'll perceive. It's excellent and prudent to stress, but when the connection suffers due to worry, it's going to be a results of neuroticism. In such a relationship, it's very hard to form things right since the neurosis always thinks of the negative side of the event than the positive side of it.

From the psychological perspective, neurotic people are believed to be more sensitive and empathetic; they have a tendency to think about other people's feelings and views as compared to other behavioral traits in society. Despite their behavior of being petty and insecure, they need a caring heart that permits them to require care of others well. Their sensitive nature makes them consider others' feelings and wishes making them liable for their wants and burdens. How does one think these people will act if one overwhelms them with many burdens? What if you complicate the requirements to the extent that they can't help anymore? Just imagine living with such people, and therefore the worry and anxiety combine thereupon of others they carry. It became more hectic to hold on with such character more so if he or she is your partner. Such a relationship is doomed to fail quite it can succeed.

Furthermore, it's worth noting that these people are generally irritable; they typically complain about anything during this world. Not that they're perfectionists, but they're worried and irritated by almost everything, making them lose contact with many of us who cannot tolerate such behavior. During a relationship, they're always nagging over anything and everything that comes their way. Such character is tough to tame, so what you are doing is tolerate or permit them the space to try to their things. The worst happens once they see any physical symptoms of illness in their body; they're going to complain about equally of it without verification from the doctor. When during a relationship with such people, it's going to be stressful to measure with them, especially once they notice any change in their general body.

Conscientiousness

Conscientiousness is taken into account to be one among the highest five personality traits. A person scoring high in conscientiousness is considered highly self-discipline. These people normally attempt to follow the plan when completing an activity, and that they don't just do things randomly like all other person. Moreover, through strict planning methodology and follow up, make them persevere, and deliver the intended result as needed. It's all about how they control, regulate, and direct their impulses towards achieving the goal objective. Besides, some individuals are considered to possess a high conscientiousness, to mean that they need a test for formulating future goal in their career. They work consistently to realize the goals set through following strict plans and organization rout to realize that in life.

However, individuals who are susceptible to score high on a test are considered the perfectionist and workaholics conscientiousness people. They will even be considered to be inflexible and boring as per their personality, which makes them busy and unavailable on social matters. Imagine they are doing not have time to spare even for the family and friends, making them be out of reach always. Once you attempt to connect with them, the probabilities of not getting their attention is extremely high once they are committed to a course of action. Through that, they're going to always make excuses to hold out their intended purposes, which makes them feel filled with life. Also, they like to be alone sometimes to specialize in their achievements and not the opposite people's demand for them. Since they're highly self-discipline, destructing them is extremely difficult, and any plan to do so may end in thwarted revocation on their part, which makes them be irritated by your action. They'll find yourself despising you for such an effort, considering the character of the task they're up to concur.

Studies show that conscientious individual trait has much to try to with impulse control than the other thing. The proactive elements of how they work make them be the way they're and not like all other personality trait. As an example, they set a timeline on how they work but not just set goals. The timeline they set is what makes them achieve the specified life goals, which make them distinctive from others, which makes them proactive and reproductive altogether their endeavors. The very fact that they follow a strict timeline makes them be the simplest productive and desirable trait as work cares. When attending an interview with these people, the likely hood of being taken for the work is extremely high. Human resource manager's skills to spot them for the task. The opposite trait that creates them more desired by the organization is their punctuality. These make them more reliable and liable for anything they typically do the maximum amount as their work cares. They're always prepared to hold out any task, which makes them more responsive and constant to the system.

Moreover, they're committed to satisfy the demand by following the tight schedule set by the organization. It's come to my attention that fewer conscience people are absolutely the other of their high conscience counterpart. They like sleeping than completing a task that needs their commitment. The less conscientious people are less productive, making them lazy on the work.

Typically, the high conscientious people are susceptible to had best when all the small print of the task are at their disposal. They follow strict instructions to the latter doing the work to be perfect and presentable when done. No wonder they're less likely to finish up behind the bar for any default within the organization. They take caution when handling anything and when it involves quality, they need nothing less but the simplest of quality to supply. In most cases, these people are regarded to be the high achievers in highschool, colleges, and the other institution where education cares. The achievement of those individuals is contributed by their cognitive ability, which makes them distinctive from the remainder. The high cognitive of most of the conscientious individuals attribute to their success in life. Besides, they typically have good relationships, work satisfaction, and achievement, which tend to land them into leadership positions at any organization. This type of trait always becomes the rule-abiding citizen who is probably going to persevere any challenges as long because it doesn't compromise their focus in life.

Openness

The openness characteristically indicates how someone is open-minded to new ideas and new things in life. An individual with this type of trait usually enjoys trying new things in life. They're not satisfied with all they need got, thus making ways to concur with other things which will seem to be beyond the reach of another individuals. These people are imaginative, curious, and open-minded, who are more susceptible to stake much on their capability on achieving certain life goals to satisfy their ego. They create it possible for everybody around them to feel that they will achieve great heights in life. Their high demanding capability and desire motivate them to be aware of every situation which needs their attention.

Moreover, they are doing not perform of these tasks alone, but they motivate other individuals within the team to realize the specified results. On the opposite hand, individuals who are low in openness usually tend to be reluctant, and that they rather not try anything new, which tries to contradict their experience and knowledge. They like to take a seat down and await things to happen in any way as long as they're not responsible. The fear of responsibility takes the higher a part of their thinking and reaction towards completing any task. How will you're taking such people to be your co-workers or partner during this challenging business world where people aren't certain about the longer term. The fear of taking risk make them undesirable, and lots of will tend to avoid them thanks to that or any undesirable trait they possess.

Furthermore, one should note that prime openness creates more opportunities for a private than low openness. The very fact that prime openness is far creative and hospitable new ideas makes them more distinct and type after by the organization in terms of employment. These people are usually imaginative and not practical, and in most cases, that's what's required on an employee who intends to blend well with the emerging economic world where the longer term is bleak and unpredictable. One must specialize in the longer term and not believe the sensible events which had occurred to get down an argument, and there are high chances that these individuals are susceptible to achieve any activity thanks to the creativity they put into practice while performing on new ventures. The likelihood of getting new ideas into practice is extremely high, making them responsible and dependable by the organization. Besides, they're always in-tuned with other people's feelings and concerns, enabling them to form good decisions for the corporate in the least times. By considering how people feel about any idea, they will deduce the simplest possible outcome which doesn't offend anyone at work. When during a brainstorming group, they're likely to return up with new ideas or develop the thought of the group member into something that folks can vouch for within the meeting. How they elaborate and visualize, the thought is so amazing that one will always fall for it. They put more specialize in the positive side of the thought and the way people are going to be ready to enjoy it, thus shedding more light on the positive perspective of it than on its negative a part of the thought.

As per the experience, openness is found to be related to a high score on intelligence. Therefore, there's how that the openness and intellect mingle to bring out a desirable result on the personality of an individual. The core existence of creativity and imaginative usually sum up the existence of an intellect factor on an individual who desires to be responsible and high achiever in life. These people are very bright and dedicated to achieving much in life as compared to a different personality trait we all know of in society. The very fact that they're innovative and artistic makes them intellectually curious and appreciative. Besides, all the innovators who have concurred the planet today have an equivalent trait, which makes them be who they're today. People like gates, Steve jobs, and Obama are open-minded to new ideas, which is what made them be who they're today. The foremost successful and respectable personality within the world today. All their success are often traced back to their openness to new ideas, influence, and challenges that they had to face before they concur with the planet we sleep in today how they strive through the challenges to form it a far better place for others to measure in and to succeed. Ever wonder how these people become more successful and influential? How they were ready to accomplice that much within the world filled with challenges, mistrust, manslaughter, and corruption everywhere.

Practically, open-minded people tend to put themselves in places or positions where they will gain new ideas, and that they value experience than the present outcome of their jobs. An open- minded person would rather choose a coffee paying job where he or she will gain much experience than choosing a high paying venture, which has already been establishing, and there's no avenue for gaining new experience out of it. These traits make them much distinct from others who will rather choose a high paying job than experience. During this times, people yearn for top paying jobs, not knowing that they will make far more money without those high paying job offers by developing their own experience to try to so. Therefore, the gap between the poor and therefore the rich is that the experience gap and not the chance gap. Everyone gets the chance to urge what they need in life, but the open-minded people check out the simplest possible experience opportunity for them to succeed and not the simplest earning opportunity. Truly, the openness to experience tend to vary through the lifespan, and in most cases, the older

people within the society tend to be less open-minded as compared to young individuals.

The Easy Way To Access Personality Types

The personality of individuals usually varies counting on the extent of engagement in daily activities starting from home, workplace, and leisure. Understanding these personality differences are often more tasking and challenging, but with clear focus and consider on the way to scrutinize them well, one can understand all of them and distinguish one from the opposite. By identifying the type of personality, one has, it's much easier to exert the influence on them and even to relate well with them without the pressure of fear of contradiction. One can capture their views, likes, and dislike equally, strike an honest relationship with these people and also communicate effectively so as to realize the best success of all time pursuit in life.

Analyzing the five personality types, including conscientiousness, extroversion, agreeableness, and neuroticism, is far important for an individual to relate well to society. Foremost, one is probably going to spot highly conscientious people to achieve success in life thanks to this type of character trait. These people tend to perform better academically, and when offered a chance to exercise their duties, they're much susceptible to be reactive and productive to the system, making them reliable. If you would like to spot this trait, search for those people that are always detail-oriented and don't like dalliance where the work cares. In most cases, they're positioned at the leadership top of the corporate to supervise the junior staff. How unlucky one are often to possess such a supervisor once you don't match their character trait is unimaginable.

Finding out the sort of personality isn't that tough for a few people, especially employers. They're going to always seek a chance to spot how the workers are thinkers or feelers to derive the distinctive character trait. Practically, thinkers will tend to form a choice supported logic, while on the opposite hand, feelers will make an equivalent decision supported the connection and values. Through these broad categories, one can identify the essential personality trait within the organization. During this case, thinkers are likely to be extroversion personality and neuroticism, while the feelers are the conscientious and openness of people. Also, one can easily identify personality types by building a relationship with these individuals. As an employer or a manager during a company, relationship matters tons, and it enables one to spot these personality traits well and help the management in pursuing goals and objectives through assigning roles consistent with the personality capability of the staff. There's a personality trait that doesn't like being managed in the least, and by realizing their existence, one can build a productive relationship where they're given an opportunity to precise themselves well. Within the end, they'll convince be more productive and realistic to realize the intended objective. An equivalent applies to non-public relationships; some people prefer lone time while others prefer a uniform company by realizing that one can know what to try to and at what time.

CHAPTER 2

THE AMAZING INNER WORLD
OF MAN

The Inner World

Everyone has an inner world that's very distinct from the surface world they encounter with their physical senses. Every emotion, thought, belief, creative imagination, dream, and fantasy you've got creates your inner world. Meaning that your inner world is defined by your imagination and your mind, the aspect of the mind not being one with the body senses. Whenever you shut off your physical sense of hearing, sight, and other senses when sleeping, you're still during a position to experience yourself as life and ready to feel in your dreams. This is often the inner world. Note that the inner world is additionally experienced through visions, intuition, imaginations, and dreams. This is often because the inner world is defined by the emotions you're feeling also as your thoughts; you are conscious within yourself.

Therefore, every doubt you've got is triggered by the planet you harbor inside you. Additionally, every fear you encounter might be your way of expressing the energy within you. We experience fear, pain, and a way of evil, not knowing that they're our own creation triggered by the wonders of our imagination. In such a state, we can't be hurt because we experience a special and private mental construct. What we provide at such some extent doesn't consider the various effects of our inner being, what it offers, also as how it influences and develops our outer life. As an example, once you are during a relationship and you're left by your partner, you tend to languish in pain. Most of the people tend to urge stuck in pain without realizing that they create the pain themselves. The inner life and beliefs are liable for creating the pain and allowing it to stay for long.

Unfortunately, most of the people are programmed to look at everything consistent with how the body behaves, with its vulnerability and pain. Some people even identify with this fact an excessive amount of that they end suffering immeasurable hurts and fear of doing things like stepping into another relationship thanks to the fear of being left by a partner and suffering the pain again. Within the inner world, we've no human body. However, most of the people just imagine themselves being within the physical world, which may be a dream of the construct they envision. But since within the inner world, we've no human body, we can't be hurt or experience pain unless we believe that we will experience the pain and hurt. Most of the people fail to understand that they need an inner world because they sleep in the outer world or what they ask because the world. They fail to understand that the inner world is what triggers them to ascertain and knowledge the outer world. People believe the outer world views that are created by the inner world as their truths. The inner world harbors all of your thoughts, beliefs, convictions and feelings. Understanding that we all have an inner world that defines how we view the outer world is usually the primary step towards understanding people also as the way to analyze them.

How does the inner world affect people's thoughts and actions?

Life may be a mirror of our inner thoughts and what's seen on the surface is that the reflection of the inner self. The thoughts we've are what makes the planet what it's, how we perceive it, and therefore the general outlook we put into it. Moreover, thought is simply a screen through which one can view your actions to depict the truth. So as to know the thoughts and actions we undertake in our daily activities, it's prudent first to research our inner being, how we behave and therefore the way we perceive things.

Interestingly, our life is that the filter of our innermost thoughts, which we integrate into our system daily. Most of the people usually think that each one their problems come from the surface world, not knowing that each one originate from within. It's important to recollect that we cannot change the planet around us, but we will change our thoughts to influence the actions of individuals within the world. Besides, aligning our thoughts with emerging issues can change things rapidly than we might imagine. One should remember that the planet is that the way it's and not as we perceive it to be. It's within us to vary what we see in ourselves and not what we see on people.

Furthermore, internal conditions usually mirror the interior self, so one should straighten the interior condition or the interior perception to settle the external disorder. You can't change the negativity you see within the world before changing the interior being, which perceives things to be negative on the surface. Change starts within no wonder pessimist has nothing positive to ascertain on people. All they see is that the negative side of the event, how that event will impact their lives, how the event makes them feel weird and not the positive things they'll enjoy from such events. Such people are hard to guide or to cooperate within an activity that needs the eye of teamwork. All they're going to neutralize the team is to seek out how on the way to alter the progress.

Similarly, there's a special mentality, which attracts different life experiences within the world, which we've to think about when making decisions. Some attract positivity, and there are those which magnetize negativity in our lives. It's the facility of belief that dictates our destiny and not the surface world which makes us who we are or the life we sleep in this world.

Typically, the predominant beliefs dictate our reality. What we expect of daylong becomes our reality through the beliefs we placed on it. Once we pray and believe that things are going to be okay within the future, through our beliefs, things tend to urge well as we perceive them to become within the near future. How does that happen? Is there any supernatural way of creating it become a reality? No, it all originates from our subconscious, our thoughts, which as perceive the event to be the truth cooperate with the forces of nature to form it's a reality. It doesn't matter what you think in or how you perceive things to be within the world. All that matters are the inner thoughts that we put into it to be what it finally become in our life. Remember that each one that we see on the surface world is our thoughts reflected on things we actually see. The funhouse we will perceive may be a results of our self-consciousness. As an example, those that were once sick within the hospitals usually become healthy again through their beliefs and mind conscious which doesn't get indulged within the effect of the illness.

The best thanks to learn more about a private is by first learning more about oneself. By doing so, one ready to be during a position to know more of the encompassing. Moreover, failure to see on the steps we take concerning our behaviors leads to a facade, and with this, learning more about others becomes difficult. If you would like to know someone, then you want to be presentable, be versed with communication skills, and your significance to the opposite individual or society members also matters. It enables you to understand yourself. As an example, if you're always sad, those around you'll always change their approach towards you, knowing alright of the results they're going to face once they're disrupting you. Additionally, if you're disciplinary, then those around you'll always change their approach towards you.

An analytical person should be conscious by having the ability to know his or her behaviors, emotions, and feelings. Being mindful enables an understanding of how people view you.

Furthermore, he results in a sincere and truthful lifestyle. An analytical person is more concerned about others' welfare, whereby when an employee in a corporation is feeling unwell, the employer should be during a position to point out kindness by letting the worker choose treatment. Analytical person's main motive is to make a peaceful environment that enhances the graceful running of projects during a business; additionally, this creates an honest understanding and a way of belonging to the minor party. People should be empathetic by having the ability to suit in other people's shoes — a way most employed by politicians when sourcing for votes from citizens. Researchers also use the technique once they want to urge information during fieldwork.

Moreover, being a part of the other's success and failures cause a robust bond of belonging and enables one to know what exactly people feel in their daily lives. An analytical person always appears sharp because he or she will observe and remember answers to previously asked questions. Furthermore, he understands the audience and knows better ways of conversation. Analytical persons always keep time on appointments, and meeting having known precisely the effects of being late affects others. One thus should get on toe so as to stay time.

In most cases, people are always prosperous since most of the time is taken on research. Good memory and enough preparation for work enable good interactions with workmates and friends. Also, proper analysis of oneself brings confidence in one before analyzing the opposite person. The analysis may convince be painful, but once this is often done, then analyzing others becomes easy.

People got to identify strengths and weaknesses for correct relations with society members. Strengths enhance socializing with people also as better communication thanks to the sensation of being loved. Moreover, an analytical person must check on better ways of curbing weaknesses because it brings about depression also as limits thinking. Depression results in anger and fear which limits progress while limiting thinking leads to a state of doubt. Therefore, this will be by taking advice from society members on better ways of improvement also as taking the initiative of change. Adopting positive thinking relieves stress.

Correspondingly, the way we perceive the planet we sleep in is as a results of our attitude expectations we put into it. In most cases, it's as a results of its dualistic nature of equal and opposite chances placed on the planet. Moreover, there's nothing like discretion because the way some people may hold it to be, but the unconscious thoughts we put into our actions, which make things to be the way they're in our life. One should remember that the inner world of ourselves is far different from the human body we encounter. From every emotions, thoughts, beliefs, fantasy, our inner imaginations are born from the inner world within us.

Each day we tend to shut our physical sense of sight, hearing, and other physical senses once we want to sleep. Why does one think human does so so as to sleep? Is there any problem if we will sleep without shutting these physical senses while sleeping? Actually, we do so unconsciously without realizing the positive impact it creates in our lives. It's during this point once we have dreams, visions, waking lucid dreams within us, and therefore the inner intuition which comes with sleep is magical. All are born from our inner being, and at these hours is when our brains tend to function well without alerting our conscious mind.

Therefore, the inner world is made by every thought we expect, every imaginations and emotion we feel our outer world, which may be seen and interpreted by people. It all originated from our consciousness, which makes our mental model to completely utilize every information which it interacts with to be realistic through perceptions. Moreover, one should note that each fear they sleep in, every doubt and self-doubts are all born from the inner self. It's with little q uestion that each fear we meet may be a results of the expressive energy we prey on it that creates it's the way it's in our life. Obviously, we will all experience fear, self-doubt, evil within the society, but all are a results of our own creations. They are doing not exist actually. It's our perceptions which breathe them life for existence and if you'll ask anybody about what you see or perceive to exists. The likelihood of getting different opinions on an equivalent subject is extremely high, which shouldn't take you all of sudden. Normally, everyone features a different mental model, and therefore the schema of everyone in society is different albeit you were born from an equivalent mother. It's nothing to try to with the genetic inheritance. That imagination, which creates devils, zombies, angels, and even external god make the planet to be the way it's today. Have you ever imagined how the planet might be if there have been no such believes that god, devils, angels, and other perceived creatures exist? In such a case, we might be living helplessly with none hope or faith that there's anything good which will happen or exists within the world.

Most of the time, we don't take many considerations of our inner self, how we perceive things and therefore the way we expect things through to precise our inner feelings. All we'd like to require into consideration is that our inner thoughts greatly influence how we act, how we react, and even how we relate with others within the community. It's not coincident that we exist;

there are a purpose and duties scheduled for us to perform on this earth and our mental model is far powerful to intervene for us.

Our inner world is all about convictions, belief, failing, fear, and therefore the ability to succeed. Most of the people specialize in the outer world, forgetting that they need the inner world which controls their thoughts, feelings, emotions, and their imaginations. By realizing this unique reality about oneself, people can do marvelous things beyond imaginations. Besides, it's the inner world that forces people to ascertain the outer world the way it's or the way we shall perceive it. The foremost influential thing about our inner world is our thoughts and therefore the perceptions we've on the outer world. There's a perception that there's another life under the bottom created to those that have gave up the ghost which is all born out of perception. All that exists is that each one the items we see on this planet ceases the instant we die, and there's nothing to aim at then. However, the believers have hope that there's life after death for the righteous people. With this belief, people have created ethical norms that regulate the conduct of everyone to act responsibly. Consistent with the bible, the assumption that there's god and life eternal after death makes us pray and believe that our tomorrow are going to be better than today. That belief is what pushes us to try to good to humanity. Ever wonder why some people are evil- minded while others are gracious and loving to their fellow men. It's the inner world they create for themselves to influence their behaviors.

The Six Basic Human Needs

In our daily walk, we tend to form decisions and take actions on the idea of what we expect, feel, and believe is vital to us. Most of the time, it's not automatic to us why we make the choice we make but the very fact is that each one folks have a singular perception that naturally places some decisions and actions over others. The planet comprises of very folks and different versions of reality unfolding daily across the planet but all of us share a crucial set of human needs that guides and motivate the choices and actions we take.

Anthony Robbins introduces the six human needs. Anthony robin has had a lifelong interest,

which he cultivated around human behavior, motivation, and development. He merged his research with neural linguistic programming, cognitive therapy, gestalt therapy, and Maslow's hierarchy of needs, and he came up with how of revolving around his believes in what he mentioned because the six core psychological needs. All folks exerting to make sure they're satisfied on an unconscious level.

In regards to Robbins, the six human needs influences a person's being's deepest motivation and determines how we rank our decisions and actions throughout our lives. The six human needs take an ascending order; this is often from a more personal and material level, to how we hook up with people and the way our interactions and energies affect the planet. All folks have phases and areas of our lives by which our focus and priorities differ. Of these needs, however, serves a crucial part in creating a life that's whole and fulfilling in the least levels. These six human needs include;

Certainty

All folks have a crucial got to satisfy their stability within the world, and it's basic. When the necessity for certainty is met at a really primary level, we are guaranteed the continuation of our dna. Certainty allows us to try to what we are alleged to do and claim certainty by having our bills and basic need covered. We even have secured relationships and movement.

It is challenging to satisfy this need because the planet and therefore the lives of the people around us are constantly changing. This causes us to put controls around our lives or remain within the temperature and resist change because it comes even when it's a healthy change. Meeting the human need for certainty involves finding or forming a way of centeredness and stability within ourselves.

Variety

There is a requirement for everybody to experience things that are far away from the norm, move from the unknown, defined and predictable in order that they will become who they need to be. The necessity to experience uncertainty, diversity, and movement tampers with the patterns of predictability and stagnation. They permit us to maneuver forward and to expand from who we are. As humans, we discover it risky to go away the world of certainty because it comes along side some comfort, but once we let it go, we enter into another level of possibility that's not governed by our past experiences.

It is difficult to satisfy the necessity for variety as long as its primary drivers are constantly changing; location, job, relationships, etc. There are times once we desire to experience the complete diversity, over time we realize that changing our external surroundings can affect our satisfying the necessity for variety and stop us from engaging with life right where we are.

Looking at it from a positive perspective, variety involves us during a balanced approach that allows us to maneuver dynamically within our outer and inner landscape and allows change when it's needed beginning with ourselves. Once we plan to create a real shift within that which must change on the surface will do so naturally without necessarily having to maneuver to a special location, a new job, or a relationship for us to experience a difference.

Significance

Every person features a got to be seen and validated for who they're and what they are doing. This need shows that we don't sleep in isolation but as a greater whole. We desire to be an efficient a part of that whole and make certain that we are playing our part well, and that we are

being appreciated for what we do on the greater whole. Once we satisfy our need for significance, we create our sense of identity during this world we sleep in.

The challenge for meeting these needs comes once we become solely hooked in to input and approval from people for us to feel complete. It's presumably a weakness in teenagers where they're constantly seeking external validation on everything they are doing. It also can be a drag if we place all our significance in one area of our lives, for instance, a job. It can get addictive and make us forsake other areas of our lives, and therefore the limits those areas can take us. Within the positive side of our got to fulfill our significance, there's a requirement for a humble sense of internal acknowledgment for following a private path of integrity and expression within the world.

Love and Connection

All folks have a requirement to feel loved in other areas, and to like others we desire to belong. The core experience we all want to realize is to possess an authentic love and deep connection n with other citizenry. An honest connection and genuine love make us have our cup overflowing and pour into the hearts of these who are around us. The shift that accompanies need resembles that of a coeliac plexus up into the guts. This is often because it takes our energy and focus beyond self-concern to form us discover the facility within the depth that tags along communing with others.

There are alternative ways during which we will express our love and reference to people. A number of the ways are healthy and balanced than others. In most cases, the perfect way and place to satisfy the fulfillment of this human need is once we first cultivate a real connection and love towards ourselves. After we experience a real connection within ourselves, we are ready to automatically hook up with people and offer them authentic love.

Growth

Every animate thing within the universe must experience growth for it to survive and thrive. May it's a micro-organism, a relationship, or an ingenious endeavor, anything that has no growth goes through stagnation and eventually dies. Growth may be a core human need, and among the primary needs that illuminates all the opposite aspects of a person's being's existence. This need are often addictive, and citizenry can take it out of balance if they are doing not roll in the hay carefully.

Growth and expansion bring a particular fulfillment to citizenry in its title that sometimes our quest to satisfy this need makes us limit ourselves from committing fully to our present lives or postpone once we can apply our growth and knowledge within the world for fear that we'd be inadequate. When fulfilling the necessity for growth, we must understand that growth doesn't occur overnight, and it's a journey, not a destination. For us to continue growing, we need to be real with ourselves and acknowledge that we aren't perfect, and that we should search for genuine ways to share what we learn and find out within the process of growth with people.

Contribution

This need involves the facility or desire of living in accordance with our purpose and bringing out the important value within the lives of people. Once we've positively attained all the opposite needs, we ascend to the present need automatically. It i expressed during a way that brings out a real sense useful within the world.

This need is brought by a basic desire for people to measure a meaningful life and to form a difference within the world we live in. It's a desire to go away a legacy and something which will be employed by future generations once we are gone. This need are often fulfilled in several ways; you'll start a foundation or volunteering group to support a cause you're hooked in to. The most challenge for fulfilling this need is that when we tap into offering genuine services to the planet, we will get overwhelmed in no time thanks to the massive number of individuals, animals, or plants that req uire that help.

Most people who have the will for contribution and giving others aren't keen to contribute to themselves. The foremost amazing expression of meeting this need comes from the belief that contribution doesn't only emanate from what we do but from who we are as people on a day to day. Once we get empowered to become our contribution within the simplest ways, then the actions that follow are related to us and therefore the power that's within us.

Prioritizing human needs

Needs are often defined because the gap that's between what's and what should be. Needs are felt by everyone, whether a gaggle of individuals, individually or maybe a community. Learning the way to prioritize needs are some things that the majority people don't know. They mostly find themselves doing the other or prioritizing the smallest amount of their needs leaving the foremost important needs. Humans have various needs and wishes that folks have differ from one person to the opposite. Therefore, it's good that we will understand other people's needs when trying to hunt out questions on their behavior. Lack of several or important needs in one's life makes them change their behaviors towards people and the way they react to different situations. It's not good to guage people from their behavior while you haven't gotten to the basis explanation for that behavior. The way people meet their needs also varies from one person to the opposite. Understanding people's behavior gives you a transparent definition of who they really are. There are alternative ways during which ready to "> you'll learn to prioritize other people's must be able to understand their behaviors at certain or given situations.

People must learn to understand and obtain to know other people's needs first to be ready to help them grow upright morally and help society at large. A pacesetter at a particular community would be worried on why their subjects became such a lot rebellious and became very abusive, which has become a threat to the community. The leader goes ahead and mobilizes people to try to a ground search from the community people and provides feedback to him on why people are behaving in such a crude manner. The people sent, gather out information from the community members by asking q uestions and getting explanations of what they have to be done. The messengers revisit to the leader, and that they lay out the people's grievances to him. The leader gets to understand that the community people feel overlooked which their needs aren't being addressed within the manner they need. In these grievances that are aired out, it's clear that 60percent of the folks that are questioned all have different needs that they need to be addressed. The leader, during this case, has got to lay out a techniq ue on the way to affect these needs and confirm that everyone feels satisfied with the strategy that has been laid out. The leader has been ready to take the primary step in understanding people's behaviors and has also been ready to know why people are acting that way within the community. By fulfilling these people's needs, the leaders will have created a particular goal that he wants to be achieved and also will help community members have a way of belonging and can feel valued. This survey conducted doesn't necessarily reveal tons of private needs but a minimum of the leader has a thought of what they ought to specialize in.

The laid out plan by the leader could focus more on solving the foremost important needs first within the community getting to the smallest amount important. However, all the requirements should be addressed since all of them are priorities. Some people won't be comfortable with how the leader has prioritized these needs since people are different and have different views. Some people may even see it fit, first of all, confirm that folks have food while others argue that they ought to first have good roads instead. This, therefore, brings another perspective that the leader has not seen. People prioritize needs differently. How people prioritize their needs create either a negative or positive consequence afterward. For instance, tom might priorities the necessity to travel watch a movie premier over the necessity to eat food. He's super hungry after the movie premier and doesn't have anything he can eat since he doesn't have any cash left on him. He now regrets getting to the films rather than eating first. People have different needs, and in each need, they need their way of solving these needs. The leader having understood the people's behavior at that moment and dealing towards achieving the answers on why they were behaving that way, helped him build a stronger bond together with his people and would now be ready to easily identify any changes in behavior from his people. This is often an equivalent way that folks should learn to know other people's behaviors first before concluding them. People are often ready to skills they prioritize their needs by watching how they answer different situations in life. This is often also an equivalent way during which we all know and obtain to know other people's needs by watching their behaviors especially situations. Prioritizing needs varies from one stage of life to a different, for instance, a toddler might see it best to stay on playing the entire day instead of eating, but as they grow, they learn that food is sweet for his or her body and hence their priority of play over food now changes to food overplay.

It is easy to understand and understand a person's need and the way they priorities it if you're employed backward from a particular situation that you simply have seen them in. Learning and understanding people's behavior helps you as an individual know the simplest thanks to help them and influence their behavior to more ethical ones. People tend to console themselves that their needs will still be there expecting them and thus, whether or not they start with the smallest amount important or the other way around, they're going to still need to solve them. The more the necessity, the more it should be prioritized, and everyone needs are important just that others aren't as important while others are often avoided. The behavior of somebody are often high thanks to their own needs, and thus, you ought to understand their behavior first, find out how they prioritize their needs then help them improve themselves.

CHAPTER 3

READING BODY LANGUAGE AT A GLANCE

The ability and knowledge that one are often ready to speed read visual communication to get lies and lesson of an individual sound awesome. The skill seems like a superhuman gift for an individual to possess and use accurately. However, it requires some patience and an open mind to develop it into its full potential. For one to interact well during a social setting, the necessity to understand the way to read visual communication is crucial. The skill enables one to interpret and understand different visual communication clues appropriately, thus getting the intended communication at the proper time amid the intended intention.

According to Igor ledochowski, an expert in visual communication teachings, he believes that one doesn't have to read thousand novels so as to become an expert in speed visual communication reading. All are born out of the intuition and not out of books. Foremost, one must keep an eye fixed on the large gesture and not the small signals emitted by an individual.

Normally, it's much to try to with keeping specialize in the opposite person and trying to trigger a spark with them. The very fact that conversation can take different avenues some may go well while others go awkwardly has much to try to with the visual communication involved within the system how the visual communication affect the overall outcome of the conversation. The signals triggered by the communicators which vary from one person to a different. Sometimes, the conversation comes with an abundance of visual communication signals that the mind cannot comprehend well thus, the necessity to research them detail by detail to succeed in a concrete conclusion is important. Besides, vesting much time on these clues is probably going to kill the conversation before it mature to its full potential. One must twiddling my thumbs with the combination signals emitted by the communicator or the listener before deriving the conclusion of what the signal might mean to the opposite party.

It is knowing stop scanning every move made by an individual while conversing, and it tends to bring an abrupt end when the person realizes that you simply are just trying to read their visual communication. Moreover, how does it feel if you're the one lecture an individual and every one they struggle to try to is to observe every move you create, the gestures and eye movement? Sometimes they are doing not consider what you're really saying. Instead, they need much interest in your limb movement and other gestures. It sounds absurd and annoying at an equivalent time, making one feel uneasy in their presence. However, it's like reading a script without noticing the most message the script is trying to convey to the audience. The very fact that you simply simply are concentrating on finer details doesn't mean that you are becoming the complete view of the message; it's rather too destructive, resulting in distortion of the intended communication message resulting in a clumsy response that can't satisfy the overall audience.

Keeping it simple enables one to catch the entire show with less pressure put in place; all you would like to try to is to specialize in the entire show and not minor details. Take a glance at the large gesture of the person you're conversing with and forget all the micro gestures which will deter you from achieving the best message.

Just in case one you're lecture is quietly dying of boredom, you're probably ready to notice the loss in eye contact, legs facing away indicating that they're close to escape or have a cross arm in their chest. Also, one must be more vigilant on the opposite signals like nodding, smiling, and engaged eye contact, signaling that somebody is proud of what you're telling them. On the opposite hand, one should take clear notice on the hand movement, in some situations, one may tend to play with hair which can clearly indicate that they're interested in you and a few extent, and that they have much interest in what you're doing than what you're doing to elicit the emotions of attraction. Some people tend to scratch their nose while thinking and it's a transparent indication that the subject of dialogue is far engaging and it requires more critical thinking than anything. The probabilities of misinterpreting these body languages are very high, and a few people usually ignore visual communication thinking that they're not a part of the conversation. When one ignores such a fundamental visual communication signal, they get out of the conversation line making them have a blurred message at the top. Nobody is prepared to clarify every detail of the conversation verbally, and albeit they will do so, the probabilities of leaving out fine details which will assist you are very high.

One must understand the law of reverse effect and be realistic that reading visual communication is primarily done by the subconscious and not for the conscious mind. One shouldn't force things on the conscious mind to read the visual communication. It's much clear that one can only read the visual communication by engaging the subconscious to interpret the facts. It happens naturally, and one doesn't have to believe it such a lot, which could complicate things. Factually, if one begins to seem into finer signals to read, they find yourself losing on the entire conversation by overthinking, and it trips up the subconscious. The likely results of the attempt it gets tongue-tied making one to distant from the conversation at the top of it all. Therefore, one should let the subconscious do what it had been meant for what it's alleged to do this makes it vital within the physical body. Getting a transparent picture of this makes one realize the elemental importance of making the avenue of mind reading and visual communication portrayal in mind. One should trust the gut instinct and not what they think it should be wish to understand a given phenomenon. Eventually, one can reach the balance of understanding of the visual communication signal without battling many facts to digest. It all depends on the instinct, which actually determines the results of the action. Through instinct, one can notice the visual communication signals and interpret them well without struggle before concluding how events are portrayed by the visual communication of an individual.

By the way, instinct doesn't just come; naturally, it's much to try to with the science of our organs, which has nerve fibers that act as a second brain in our body. They typically send the right signal to the brain from the interpretation of what's happening on the surface or once we are conversing with people. An individual who can follow the gut instinct stands a far better chance of getting full notice of everything going around them, thus making them more active and sensitive to different life events. Therefore, the necessity to urge a full conversation edge depends on the instinctive gut arising from the subconscious of an individual. Following your gut enable one to urge full information from different a part of "> a part of the body accessed by the capacity of the subconscious part of the brain.

Also, it helps one to interact the entire mental model while thinking and reasoning process which is crucial for existence during this world. It shows that the gut is liable for reasoning and knowledge processing.

One crucial way of letting our instincts to hurry read the visual communication are often accelerated by being asleep with the discomfort. One can easily interpret the visual communication by relaxing during a discomfort situation or through tension.

Such situations tend to supply a car window of how things are to an individual. One can easily identify defaults and lacking during a person during these moments. By having mindful breathing, one can link to the prefrontal cortex liable for breathing regulation, thus providing the essential condition. Breathing turns off the panic, which can overwhelm one to be distressed and act awkwardly. People indeed incline to act abnormally when faced with problems that they can't bear. Turning off such temptation through cautious breathing through the nose and slightly making some breath out through the mouth eases the strain and pressure on the brain creating a conducive atmosphere suitable for focusing.

Sometimes people might not be receptive to what you've got to inform them, or they are doing not create attention to the conversation. These are often contributed by the perceived intention of the conversation, thus leading them to possess that countenance. Have you ever ever encountered a salesman trying to sell for you an item you've got no interest in at all? How does it feel once they attempt to persuade you to shop for such items knowing well that you simply don't need it within the first place? Nevertheless, they have a tendency to urge attention clumsily without realizing the impact of their actions at the top. One can purchase from them without noticing that that they had bought what they didn't need. The facility of visual communication reading plays an important role during this. They only snap you out of a particular behavior without realizing it. All they are doing is to maximize that behavior to solicit more feelings and interest in you. The friendly switching way makes one friendly and submissive to their trap thus making one be ready to buy from them. These people have perfected visual communication reading; they skills to tune you to their way of thinking. If we could all learn an equivalent skill, people could make great heights in life. Imagine trekking up the road to strike a conversation with a stranger without being intimidated about what they consider you or what your actions will mean to them.

Typically, smiling can portray tons about the emotions and the way one takes the knowledge given to them. The mouth can lie while someone is smiling and portray other feelings aside from being happy, but the eyes cannot give fault impression. Once you are having a conversation with an individual and realize that there's a crinkling of skin around their eyes, it indicates that they're genuinely involved within the conversation, and that they are pleased with the subject. In most cases, people always smile to cover true feelings, and once you are an honest observer, you'll realize the deceit more easily without much ado. One can smile through the mouth and show no expression on the face making it deceitful. Therefore, next time you're conversing with another party, pay much attention to the smile, and if it doesn't show on the face through the wrinkle, make certain that it's not genuine, and you're just being deceived. These people might be hiding something which they are doing not want you to understand, and perhaps it's something sensitive that they are doing not want you to note. In such circumstances, attempt to be vigilant on how they talk; the wording tends to betray their true feelings making them more vulnerable once they cannot hide it anymore. Getting a full view of these feelings and deception makes one wise of the environment during which they perform the conversation. Ever wonder why some people are going to be shy and always find an excuse to seem away while lecture you. What they always feel uneasy around you, and once you attempt to confront them, they typically fake a smile pretending that everything is okay, yet they're not. Get the complete picture of that one that is usually pretending to smile will ask, but the smile usually lasts for a couple of seconds? He will always be at any slight provocation of pleasure, even when that excitement doesn't exist. What's the sensation of lecture such people? How does one portray what they tell you? Does one think they're genuine or one? The eyes tell it all though to some people you can't judge supported the attention gesture, and you've got to mix it with other visual communication signals.

Ever been during a meeting and see that somebody is trying to imitate your body movement, that each time you cross or uncross your legs that do an equivalent in response. Once you tilt your head, they too do an equivalent way as you are doing. This type of gesture may be a good sign of visual communication; they're just trying to mirror body language unconsciously. In real sense, you'll think that they're copying what you're doing, but they're much unaware of what's happening too. It's a receptive language indicating that they're conscious of what you're doing and fully engaged within the conversation that they lose self-awareness of what's happening in their bodies. They only answer nature and not imitating what you're doing. Any plan to disrupt their visual communication may cause loss of concentration and even loss of interest on the subject of dialogue. Therefore, the simplest thing to try to is to allow them to be as they're and do what pleases them. You never know; they will be the simplest partner during a business dealing you plan to initiate within the future.

If you're conversant in a corporation structure, whenever you walk into a replacement corporate, you'll easily identify the person responsible once they walk into the space. One can only realize that from the visual communication, the person emits and not the words they assert sometimes. The erect posture, open and expansive gesture portrayed by the person can tell the sense of authority of an individual. One doesn't need an evidence or to be told that somebody may be a leader, just from the visual communication, you'll be ready to get the complete information you need. How one maximizes the space they fill makes it evident that they're in authority or that they hold a superiority position in a corporation. It's true that when an individual maintains an honest posture, he commands much respect and engagement albeit you're not a pacesetter. This visual communication posture is to insinuate that folks with good posture depict confidence and determination towards achieving their goals in life. With this data, one are often ready to employ a competent employee deriving from the character and visual communication which shows that they're dependable.

Ultimately, there's a notion that the attention doesn't lie. Have you ever wondered why most of the people enforce being looked into the attention when having a conversation? What can that mean to you? The overall perception of the attention contact is that it tells all and anyone lying will never keep an honest eye contact lest he or she wants to be ungrounded by the lie they tell. However, some people will hold eye contact deliberately to hide up for the lie. On the opposite hand, unblinking stare also can be intimidating, and it makes one feel uncomfortable sometimes. One should, therefore, know to differentiate an honest gaze from the dishonest gaze.

The Secrets of Non-Verbal Communication

We do communicate with each other not only through verbal communication but also through non-verbal communication cues like eye contact, posture, and eye gesture. These other body languages portray quite what we communicate verbally. Traditionally, people didn't use spoken or written way of expression. Non-verbal communication has existed since eternity. How does one express yourself to an individual who doesn't understand your language, more so once you attend a far off land where you are doing not know anybody who can interpret for you anything? Getting the knowledge across is that the objective of all communication. Since everyone desires this, they're going to do anything to form themselves be understood through various means possible. Long before the written communication evolves, most of our forefathers use non-verbal communication skills to pass a message across.

Sincerely, words aren't always aligned with the non-verbal clues people always associate them with. In most cases, people speak, but their visual communication indicates other words. Understanding these non-verbal skills creates an avenue for increased understanding when conversing with an individual over a problem. It gives the proper impression of what to expect, what to mention next when talking, and the way to relate to people generally. Without such skills, a stimulating mixed message may lose its meaning when it can't be translated within the right way possible.

Moreover, there's much happening with our emotions, which aren't rightly expressed through verbal communication. What we expect or feel aren't always voiced when communicating. Ever wonder why some people will always beg others to inform them what's wrong with them, how they feel about something, or their opinion once they can depict that there's something wrong, but they are doing not realize it. The inner feelings are hidden within us unless we mention it publicly. To some extent, there's how of showing this non-verbal secret to the overall public, how they affect one, and the way one can interact with them effectively to bring out the meaning. You'll argue that one can still communicate through digital platforms like social media and the other platform.

Nevertheless, visual communication are often amid the variation of voice tone, eye contact, and body movement which may help one to spot the meaning. In other words, social media platforms cannot reveal truth feelings of an individual unless he talks his or her mind bent the general public. Anyone conscious of what the non-verbal communication reveals about their feelings, thoughts, and perceptions towards a given subject will always be aware of its use and the way it should be expressed. He or she is going to always work on the clues and stop sending the incorrect message to people that may ruin their reputation at the top of it all. Therefore, having a self-evaluation put one a notch above the remainder during this caliber. It gives you an opportunity to be better than others within the group setting.

Sometimes one cannot avoid frowning or squinting when to speak. These sorts of facial expressions reveal tons a few person than we usually notice on the surface; it really tells what's happening inside an individual, how they feel inside their heart and mind. Besides, this countenance can't be avoided when communicating, making them an important a part of communication. Imagine someone communicating with an expressionless look which indicates that somebody isn't curious about the conversation. It shows how one is bored and has no much interest within the talk you're engaging them in, and to some extent, you're just wasting their precious time, which they might have employ elsewhere to get more income. The countenance vividly shows the intention and therefore the perception behind every communication outcome of an individual. One can see a fake deceptive smile through countenance. When this expression doesn't match the verbal message being conveyed, one can easily influence the listener without much ado with little perception configured to make the intended message.

On the contrary, one can examine the attention contact made during the conversation to form a transparent clue of what's happening. Remember, eyes are the conceivable windows to the soul, and thru eyes, one can easily predict what's happening in your heart, how you are feeling, and therefore the perception you've got towards a given subject. Have you ever imagined that through your eyes, one can tell the type of an individual you're and therefore the character you carry around? Consider that next time you're having a conversation with another person; how they take you matters tons, which is predicated on the type of eye contact you retain with them during conversation. Moreover, lack of eye contact when conversing may be a sure clue that you simply can't be trusted by anything under the sun. It doesn't matter how great you're at the presentation once you keep it up watching the ground throughout the presentation process. The perception of being unconfident, shy, and nervousness can't be erased by anything, but the attention contact one keeps during a presentation.

If there's anything which will betray you when talking is your hands. How does one use them to portray a message, what movement do they create once you are lecture someone? The hand secrets aren't known to several people, but it's time to handle them well when conversing with someone next time. Moreover, it can reveal confidence, fear, stress, etc. People will assume you counting on how you employ your hands while communicating. As an example, in western culture, handshake is considered a symbol of respect, and it's highly encouraging when communicating with someone. When it's amid direct eye contact once you meet one for the primary time, respect is earned, and other people view you as a virtue's person in society.

Nevertheless, when it's not been expressed appropriately, people tend to require you without any consideration sort of a joker who isn't serious. To people, a weak handshake is considered being disinterested within the subject or business you're close to transact. Besides, who will search for a fragile person with a weak personality as a partner within the business dealing? It doesn't appeal to people within the western culture where most of the business person must be daring and innovative to undertake new things. Steady and dry handshake implies that you simply are confident and reliable since it matches the strength of the person offering the deal within the first place.

On the opposite hand, an open hand while talking generally indicates that you simply are an open-minded person with a relaxed personality. This type of fact must be kept by people that tend to succeed during the recruitment process. The human resource panel looks at these signs to derive the simplest candidate for the work they're close to offer. Interestingly, these visual communication signs are much important to the interviewer when evaluating the simplest candidate, thus keeping them in mind enable one to achieve success in such a situation once they encounter one. How does it feel to be the simplest candidate for employment when all the interviewer get right from you may be a great visual communication gesture that doesn't match others? In some instances, one may have an identical qualification with others, then it reaches some extent once they had to seem at the opposite factors to differentiate the candidate's potential. Never underestimate the facility of visual communication more so hands when lecture anyone from now henceforth.

Furthermore, the communicator tone of voice usually tends to interrupt or make a message successful while communicating with people. One should be ready to distinguish between soft voice and hard voice when to use them when conversing. One can say word in an honest requesting intention, but the tone of the voice may betray the message intended. Some people will take as being arrogant or demanding during a certain way that shows that you simply didn't shall be polite within the first place. In such a situation, one will always an impolite answer consistent with the initial tone sound. As an example, "come here" are often an invitation and a requirement counting on the voice tone employed by the person requesting or demanding for the opposite person to return where they're, which is how the intention is misplaced. Once you use a yelling and aggravating tone, it only indicates that you simply aren't pleased with things, and therefore the intention is to harm the one you're yelling. The irritating voice tone only indicates conflict or the likelihood of erupting conflict with an individual on the brink of you to urge what you would like. It doesn't matter how good it's going to sound, but the instant you're shouting to an individual, the message will never be pleasant for his or her ears or to anyone within the environment.

It is knowing emphasize the words you chose while communicating to dramatize their importance and therefore the emergency, which comes with the message. By doing so, one can analyze the type of message and therefore the importance it's on you. The type of voice you employ while conveying the message sum it all. It shows that you simply care about the listener once you use a soft and requesting gesture when communicating with the opposite person. The context of the message can vary from one listener to a different, but the way you portray your message, the way it's modeled before being released for audience consumption matters tons.

Moreover, eye-blocking, a commonly witnessed non-verbal communication vice, can decipher that an individual is threatened by a particular situation or event. In most young adults, one are often seen closing their eyes in order that they are doing not witness something. In most cases, it shows how shy an individual is and therefore the fear to concur that fear resulting in the closing of the eyes. These sorts of nonverbal communication are much common in people that don't want to precise themselves publicly or a given situation resulting in dejection and self-denial a few given idea or circumstance.

The investigation conducted to determine how the blocking of the attention while communicating shows that it works alright with many of us. As an example, there was a robbery during a certain company, and therefore the investigators came in to interrogate the possible intruders. In their first interrogation session, they req uest to start out with the watchman who was guarding the building. That they had three inq uiries to ask the watchman, which had to offer a cause possible intruders' whereabouts. Foremost, they begin with what the watchman saw before the incident, then where he was at the time when the incident occurs, but before proceeding to subseq uent q uestion, they realize that the guard blocks his eyes. There and there, they realize that there's something there to try to with the whereabouts of the guard at the time of the incident. To harmonize the entire process to its perspective, they realize that there's an opportunity that the guard wasn't around at his spot at that hour of the incident. Factually, the guard wasn't around at the time of the theft, he visited sleep reception, and when he returned later, he acknowledged that the occurrence has taken place.

In this case, the visual communication of the guard gave him away. By blocking his eyes, the detectives were ready to detect the mischief in him. He was guilty of not being where he was alleged to be at the occurrence of the incident, and therefore the guiltiness digs deep in him, thus confusing witnessed. He feels that he's liable for the tragic theft witnessed at the shop and there could be other fear of losing the work at the shop making him miserable at an equivalent time. In most cases, one are often too convincing by using the verbal communication sort of portraying the message, but to some extent, the message are often contradicted by the non-verbal communication techniques which don't match what one is saying. What percentage times have you ever been cheated or cheat someone about something, and your hand and body gesture portray something else? At one point, I used to be telling somebody how great the place I visited was wonderful and therefore the way I enjoy staying at that place. All this long, i had no sort of excitement in my face and didn't realize how unrealistic I sounded till one among my best friends, who was among the audience, drags me apart and tells me on my face that I'm lying. From that day, i realize how crucial the non-verbal communication gesture means to people. Imagine how these people are silent and watching every move I made with my eyes, hands, and legs, how the story sounds awkward to them, and therefore the quite patience they place into that story only to understand that it had been just a pass time fun story which never happened. If it had been you, how will you're taking me? I do know the solution you have; you'll never trust me again even next time when am genuine about something. This shows how one can lose respect while trying to amuse friends or to form an occasion enjoyable for people on the brink of you during a given setting.

Ultimately, there are great danger people make once they cannot use the proper tone while communicating, which tend to portray among the professionals. The inflection in your statement matters tons to folks that what you're actually saying. It's within the voice that says that message that matters to people. How will you convince one if you can't convince yourself that what you're saying convince your inner being? How does it cause you to feel when it's actualized? How does the potential outcome affect your whole being? Is there any passion for what you're trying to mention otherwise you are just saying it for the sake of profit? What many of us don't realize is that the impact of the message can only be realized when there's a force behind it that propels its actualization. The eagerness in your eyes, how you stress something to derive the particular meaning. In fact, how will you convince potential investors to place their money during a project that doesn't elicit their interest? The way you portray the possible profit and therefore the other benefits that it'll accompany matters tons. I don't advocate for cheating or exaggeration of the facts to suit your needs during this case, but being honest is that the key. An excellent communicator must skills to use tonal variation, eye contact, and hands well while painting the message picture to the audience for visualization. When the audience can visualize the particular picture in their minds, they're going to eventually buy that concept albeit it's not realistic to others.

CHAPTER 4

RECOGNIZING LIERS

A lie are often defined as an assertion that's believed to be forced to easily deceive somebody. Lies involve a spread of interpersonal and psychological functions for the people that use them. People use lies for various reasons which are, at the most times, best known to them only. It's believed that each person can lie. Multiple sorts of research have suggested that on a mean day, people tell one or two lies each day. Some surveys have suggested that 96 percent of individuals admitted to telling a lie sometimes while 60 percent of a search study wiped out the claimed that they are doing not lie in the least. However, the researchers found a minimum of half that number were lying. However, scientists say that there are ways during which one can easily spot a lie or be ready to know when somebody is lying to you. Lies are often intended to guard someone while others are very serious like covering up a criminal offense done. People don't know what ways they will use to detect a lie, and most of them find yourself telling themselves that they will easily detect a lie. You'll easily recognize a lie by noting down the nonverbal cues that folks use like for instance, a liar cannot look you directly within the eye; however, researchers have proven that this won't necessarily work. In 2006, bond and de Pablo acknowledged that only 54 percent of individuals were ready to detect a dwell a laboratory setting. Investigators also don't find it easy to detect a lie and may easily be fooled into believing what's not. Most of the people believe that trusting your instincts always is that the best thanks to avoid being fooled.

Gesture

This is a sort of nonverbal communication where body actions tend to talk or communicate particular messages. Gestures include the movement of hands, feet, face, and other body parts. Gestures enable one to speak non-verbally to precise a spread of feelings and thoughts. For instance, people can communicate none verbally once they are in trouble and wish somebody's help. The gesturing process comes from the brain which is employed by speech and signing. It's believed that language came from manual gestures that were being sued by the Homo sapiens. This theory is understood because the gestural theory that was caused by the renowned philosopher abbe de condillac within the 18th century. However, the utilization of gestures are often how to notice when somebody is lying to you. Some people find it hard to regulate their body motions when telling a lie. That's why gestures are wont to detect when somebody is lying to you. Different body expressions will tell you when an individual is lying.

The mouth cover

This gesture has been at the most times utilized in childhood. An individual lying to you'll cover their mouth when trying to stop themselves from saying the deceitful words. Most of the people don't entirely cover their mouths but use just a couple of fingers covering the lips. People may attempt to fake a cough to be ready to get an opportunity to hide their mouths, which by the way, doesn't make any difference whether or not they cover it fully or partly. However, this gesture must be carefully examined before concluding that the person is lying. If the person covering the mouth is that the one talking then it's presumably that they're those lying and if the one covering the mouth is that the one listening then this could be a show that they're carefully taking note of what's being said and could be probably thinking that you simply are totally not sincere with them. People that can note this behavior can't be easily fooled or manipulated or controlled in any way. The liar will always be scared of approaching the person since they're afraid that their intentions will easily be noticed. This reduces the speed at which individuals use others to their advantage thereby influencing the community ethically.

The nose touch

Most people that lie tend to always touch their nose while talking. After letting go of their mouth, they have a tendency to the touch their nose and check out to fake that they're itching. It's almost instant to notice when it's just a traditional nose itch or when someone is trying to use it to cover a lie. A traditional itch are often relieved q uickly by just an easy scratch, but if someone keeps on scratching and touching their noses, meaning that they're lying.

The eye rub

The brain tends to use the attention trick as how of hiding deceit. People that lie tend to rub their eyes to cover the clear show from their eyes that they're lying. Tons of individuals find it difficult to take care of eye contact once they are lying, and that they tend to keep off whenever they appear at the person they're lying to. They, therefore, rub their eyes to cover from the very fact that they're lying. People say that the eyes tend to make a symbol of doubt to the person you're lecture. This is often why most of the people rub their eyes to cover this sign.it is said that men roll in the hay very vigorously while women roll in the hay gently without having to harm themselves much. Having the ability to acknowledge this gesture will help the community and society at large to be ready to repel liars.

The ear grab

When an individual is lying, they have a tendency to the touch and fiddle with their ear lobe as they talk. This makes one feel a touch easier while telling a lie and also trying to dam themselves from hearing the words that they're saying. Children tend to hide their eyes once they hear something they think may be a lie, and that they don't want to listen to it.

Neck scratch and other body parts

Adults who lie tend to use their index for scratching their neck slightly below their ear lobe. This is often done a couple of times, showing that the person is lying. An individual who is lying tends to also put a finger within the mouth once they feel they're under tons of pressure. Lying creates a really uncomfortable state for people and that they, therefore, are unable to regulate their feelings round the people they're lying to.

Change in breathing and therefore the collar pull

This gesture art was first discovered by desmond morris when he noticed that there's always a tingling sensation within the facial and neck tissues, which causes one to rub or scratch that place a few of times. The increased vital sign brings about the sweating of the palms and sometimes even under the armpits. This causes you to in need of breath once you start suspecting that the person you're deceiving won't be believing you. This is often called a reflex action.

The position change of the top

People do tend to form quick and sudden head movements after they need been given an immediate question or query, they're likely too be lying about something. They're going to either retract the top, or it'll face downwards or maybe titled to at least one side before they answer the question you had asked them.

Feet shuffling, holding a stare and standing still

People who aren't moving in the least once you engage during a conversation with them should be a involve concern. It's normal that once you two people converse, there's movement of the body during a relaxed way, but if the opposite person is extremely rigid and seems relaxed during a very extraordinary way could show that probably there's something very off that person. The shuffling of the feet is caused by being nervous and uncomfortable. It could also show that the person eagerly wants to go away the conversation as soon as possible. Watching an individual's feet and their movements tell you tons about what that person is saying. It's renowned that the majority people are unable to take care of eye contact when lying; however, another people don't move an eye fixed or blink once they are lying to you during a quest to completely pull you off with their lie and manipulation. Liars tend to use a chilly stare when trying to intimidate and control you.

The above-explained gestures are seen during a lot of individuals that attempt to manipulate people or mislead them to urge what they need. However, it's good if you all have these skills which will assist you in identifying folks that fiddle together with your mind or might want to use yours to your advantage. Most of the people who lie will lack words to mention since all their tactics are revealed and learned by everyone.

Facial expressions

The facial expressions that an individual makes tell you tons, whether or not they are lying or not. Lies to you become obvious once you can learn these different cues during a conversation. All that goes around someone's face shows either dishonesty or honesty during a conversation. The subsequent are the facial expressions which will tell you that an individual is lying.

The eyes

The eyes are what most of the people use to notice whether the opposite person is telling the reality or they're just lying. The eyes create a link to both imagination and memory. Imagination is usually seen as an honest thing when one is creating a lie. This is often because one is in a position to imagine situations in their head and also attempt to find out the reaction of that person after they hear the lie.it is said that when an individual looks up to and to the left after being asked an issue, they're usually trying to recall some information where the memory comes in. This act is usually told to be the reality. When someone looks up and to the proper, they're utilizing their imagination or in other words, fabricating information to offer to you. This is often taken as a lie. After asking an issue pay close attention to the person's eyes and which direction they move. The eyebrows also tend to boost once they are telling the reality and have a tendency to blink or close their eyes tons to steal time for them to rethink their lie and confirm that their story is kept intact without having to betray themselves through the eyes. Most of the people that lie also tend to avoid eye contact with the person they're lecture. When forced to form eye contact, they often feel uncomfortable and should even come short of words making the opposite person now that they were trying to mislead them.

Blushing

When an individual is telling a lie, they have a tendency to often blush. They become nervous thereby creating a rise within the blood heat, especially round the face area. Blood tends to flow within the cheeks thereby causing the liar to blush or recoil. Although blushing are often stimulated by a few of the many other things, it's almost certain for a liar to blush. This could be an honest way also to understand when somebody is blushing.

Smiling

A person that lies while smiling doesn't have tons of facial expressions just like the flickering of the eyes to point out that their smile is real. However, liars smile with "dead eyes" that don't brighten up their faces. A true smile features a great effect on the eyes and tends to cause the eyes to either become big or small. This is often because more muscles are utilized in becoming happy instead of forced demands. A liar always features a fake smile whereby the reality of their lie is revealed by their eyes once more. Having the ability to differentiate between a true and faux smile will assist you in distinguishing between an individual who is telling the reality and one who is lying.

Micro expressions

Facial expressions that easily come and go quickly function best indicators that an individual could be lying. These expressions are referred to as micro expressions. These expressions convince be great lie detectors and reveal the raw truth. These expressions also reveal if there's something wrong since it's hard to cover these expressions. However, it's good to notice that not all micro expressions reveal that an individual is lying this is often why it's highly advised that you simply be trained on how best to notice and differentiate these feelings. Before concluding that the person you're questioning is lying it's advisable that you simply first check on the circumstance and situation at hand.

Speech

The way an individual speaks while ahead of you'll tell tons in terms of truth and lies. Liars tend to repeat themselves tons while speaking because they're unsure of what they're saying and are struggling to convince themselves of their lives. An individual who is lying to you tends to talk during an in no time way which enables them to bring out the lies during an in no time and consistent way. They're often left wondering whether the lie they told would be believable causing them to possess a rise in heartbeats. Liars tend to feature more or extra details to their stories to be ready to convince their listeners that what they're saying is true. They take brief moments to rehearse or re-evaluate the answers that they had rehearsed before to make sure that they are doing not make any mistake which will make their listeners doubt them. They sometimes become defensive about their answers and also tend to play the victim if they think their lie isn't going as that they had planned. However, the liar doesn't stand an opportunity if the person telling lies has an expertise in understanding and knowing when an individual is lying to them or when trying to make a lie.

The direction of the eyes

People who might not be telling the reality may tend to seem to the left to construct or create imagery in their heads. Looking up and to the proper is taken into account to be an attempt to undertake and remember something that happened which is true as compared to looking up and to the left which is taken into account as trying to make a lie through imagination. However, this could be a touch bit confusing for those folks that are left-handed. Left-handed people tend to try to the other of this theory, they appear up and to the proper when trying to make a lie and appearance up and to the left when trying to recollect some events that took part within the past. The left side of a left-handed person is taken into account true while the proper side is taken into account to be a lie.

Voice change

Gregg mccrary, a retired federal bureau of investigations criminal profiler, stated that a person's voice might change abruptly once they tell a lie. This strategy works by first noting their speech patterns by asking simple questions for instance, where they live. By this one can monitor the varied changes within the speaking tones once they are faced with a tougher question. An individual who learns this art can easily tell when an individual is telling or trying to make a lie.

The facial expressions explain above clearly show that folks must learn these arts to be ready to affect people within the society who love manipulating others. These people tend to confuse people by lying to them and making these lies true in order that they will escape with their lies. An individual who isn't ready to identify such sorts of people is at a better risk of getting blackmailed by these people and making you are doing want they need to try to, for instance, commit a criminal offense for them.

Word Choice

Liars have a really good selection of words and that they are very careful with the words they chose to use with their fabricated stories. Philosophers say that lying is tough work since it involves tons of thinking and nut-cracking to make sure that your story looks true and not in any way imagined. Convincing someone with a lie requires you to possess the story straight and it should be accompanied with the proper choice of words and visual communication. People that don't skills to acknowledge liars require to find out this art first while liars should rehearse their lines properly before telling it to people. Liars have ways during which they will convince you of the reality. These ways are discussed down below.

Liars repeat an issue verbatim

This is an art that liars use to assist them delay to organize themselves to answer your question. During a normal conversation, people repeat almost half the questions but liars tend to repeat the entire question which could seem awkward and bizarre to the person interrogating them. If this person is keen, they're going to be ready to note that they're being lied to. For instance, hi john, did you send the message to the staff supervisor? John be the liar, during this case, will respond, did i send the message to the staff supervisor? This immediately tells you that the person is intentionally buying enough time to possess fabricated a story for.

Liars take a guarded tone

Liars always tend to form a significant guarded approach to the people questioning them and make it appear as if the person questioning them doesn't know what they're saying. Taking into reference the instance given above, if john had responded as, what does one mean? This might sound a touch guarded and offline but john is simply trying to hide up a lie by making the opposite person look bad for asking them the question and not trusting them. A suspicious reply to an issue is uncalled for whether it had been the reality or not and this might indicate that you simply try to cover some dwell there between.

Liars use non-contacted words in their denial

The choice of words employed by liars while denying an allegation tends to sell them up to their interrogators. Using the words like, i did not, rather than didn't would bring tons of emphasis into your statements which can show the others that you simply try to stress things especially which even wouldn't be important within the first place. They have a tendency to mention quite they realize with their words. Liars also tend to form sure that's very particular in what they assert and choose their words very carefully ensuring that they are doing not implicate themselves in their talk. People that are telling the reality, however, don't strain to offer out specific details about themselves goodbye as they're telling the reality.

Use of strict chronology

Liars tend to stay their information up so far and that they don't want even one detail rupture of place. They, therefore, tend to use chronological accounts when concerning events. However, people that are truthful and aren't telling lies tell their stories with how they clearly remember the events that happened. Liars, on the opposite hand, make their stories strictly in chronological order and that they strictly want people to concentrate and believe their stories.

Euphemisms

It is attribute to not want to implicate themselves in doing the incorrect things or being caught on the bad side of the law. Liars, therefore, tend to use this nature to urge faraway from what they're being accused of. They, therefore, tend to reply to the question during a more relaxed and soft manner which will leave you thinking that they didn't do what you'll be accusing them of. For instance, did you steal the cash that i had kept in my purse, the respondent during this case who is additionally the liar will respond, i didn't take it?

Liars overemphasize their truthfulness

Most liars tend to always use words which will cause you to believe whatever story they're telling you to be true. The utilization of words like i swear, believe me, to inform you the reality, i8 promise and lots of others will show you that the storyteller wants you to badly believe the knowledge they're supplying you with to be true. People telling the reality don't use such statements or words to undertake and show their honesty they simply say it and leave it to you to either believe them or leave it. It's very easy to understand when someone is lying to you if they keep it up repeating and emphasizing their truth.

Liars tend to avoid pronouns

In normal conversations, it's normal to use quite fair amount of pronouns in between the conversation. But liars try the maximum amount to avoid the utilization of pronouns in their conversations. They struggle the maximum amount as possible to be extra careful with their words. They have a tendency to use the person more rather than specifying and using the primary person where applicable. For instance, a liar may say, you are doing not engage in extracurricular activities if you are doing not want to rather than i don't engage in extracurricular activities because I do not want to. During this case, they do not want it to be revealed that they're talking about themselves in real sense.

Liars hedge their statements

This is mostly characterized by people within the courtroom or political hearings. These people tend to use statements like, as far as i can recall, if you think that about it, what i remember is, these statements are employed by people that try to cover something and are probably on a hot seat or interrogations. People that are giving out truthful information don't use such phrases and have a tendency to only go straight to the purpose and answer the questions they're being asked.

Liars use long introductions and skip main events

People who lie tend to require an excessive amount of time introducing themselves or introduc9ing the subject they need to debate therefore leaving out the important details within the conversation. This helps them build credibility in their story padding it with tons of factual content the maximum amount as they will. A researcher acknowledged that an individual telling a lie is probably going to feature more details on themselves but lack words when it involves the most a part of the story. Careful listeners are likely to notice this beforehand and may tell that the person is lying to them. They will easily find missing details within the story being told.

Liars are very careful about the selection of words they use and thus if people don't know the proper thanks to distinguish these words, they'll find yourself being manipulated and being taken for a fool. Having the ability to differentiate between a lie and therefore the truth will help tons.

Speech Patterns

These are distinctive ways of oral expression. Liars tend to possess different speech patterns once they lie and thus, they're very careful when speaking ahead of individuals. To be ready to beat a liar at their own game, the key is usually to concentrate attentively to what they're saying. A search team from the University of Arizona led by judee burgoon analyzed the speech of corporate fraudsters.

They went through over 1,000 statements that had been made by the ceo and cfo of 1 company during their quarterly conference calls. These companies had been evicted as a results of fraud in several lawsuits. The researchers were ready to compare between the scripted and unscripted speech.

The research team acknowledged that it might be easier to dwell cognitive taxing instead of telling the reality. During a lie, a really simple language is employed to make sure that the liar doesn't complicate issues with their own words. They stated that it might be hard for the human mind to take care of a false story and are available up with connecting linguistics utterances thanks to the increased cognitive load on the human brain.

This is why liars use an easier language to avoid confusing themselves. It had been previously discovered that folks who lie distant themselves from their lies. They use short and vague statements like maybe, i guess, and so on. They also tend to avoid using the primary person singular pronoun in their accent, for instance, i, me and myself which show actual ownership of the statement getting used. It also should be noted that liars tend to talk q uite natural. They have a tendency to feature more details to their story to convince you that what they're saying is true. They are doing not like silent pauses or silence in their conversations and that they wish to keep it going and going.

A financial expert was delivered to help encode the overstatements and lies that were associated with financial fraud. Special software was wont to analyze call recordings from the calls at a granular level to assist differentiate the lies and therefore the truth.it was confirmed that certain speech patterns were used while the executives were lying. The fraud-related speech recorded was fuzzy, more hedged words were used.

The researchers also acknowledged that fraudulent speeches attended be longer and more detailed than the honest ones. The executives used more positive words than the negative ones in their talk, suggesting how they ought to twist to a more positive spin to what was being reported. This research proved that it's very easy to notice the speech patterns of varied people or liars who would want to cover something that they might not love known to people also.

This research showed that noting down the speech patterns and having the ability to acknowledge when somebody is telling a lie would help the society ethically to be ready to establish a number of this stuff like crime and fraud in companies. It might also help know people that would really like to use people to their advantage or might want them to try to regrettable things beat the name of pleasing them. If you are feeling that somebody could be lying to you, try the maximum amount and alter the subject and note the sudden change within the one that was telling a lie. They become more relaxed and cozy within the new topic that you simply mentioned. An individual who doesn't know this could be confused and would want to travel back to the previous discussion since it had been cut abruptly and with no warning.

The liar would also want to use humor and sarcasm in ask hide their lie by making it seem kind of funny. It's also been seen that folks who lie tend to point tons. They use their fingers to point on to something to distract you from thinking what they're saying or making you remove your mind from whatever lies they're telling you in order that they feel easier in telling a lie. They have a tendency to point during a different direction aside from within the direction they're watching this may clearly show you that the person is telling you a lie. However, there some people that naturally like using gestures as they talk and this for them should be no cause for alarm since this is often how they're and it might be hard changing them.

Most people don't like conversing with people that like using gestures in their talk since they find it ir6ritating and it's also very hard to understand when that person is lying to you. People that use gestures particularly the hands can easily lie and therefore the lie goes unnoticed if the people around him aren't too keen on what he's saying.

Not all people that exhibit these signs are liars some are just naturally like that. Therefore, the above behaviors should be compared thereto person in their current and normal situations. Some people naturally cannot maintain eye contact because they're shy, others cannot make complete sentences without having to flutter their feet, and thus as you inspect for liars it's also good to notice that people are naturally that way.

Lie detectors or experts in detecting lies claim that a mixture of visual communication and other cues whether verbal or non-verbal should be utilized in determining whether somebody is telling the reality or not. The society should also come up with ways to affect people that mislead escape with crimes that they need committed. They ought to confirm that folks who lie whether with good or bad intentions should be puni8shed and addressed properly.

The society would be an honest place to measure in without people that lie and have a tendency to control others with their lies. People lie all the time and, altogether places, and thus it's good to notice once you are during a place that needs total honesty and truth. Having these crucial lie detectors at7 the rear of your mind will assist you know easily when somebody is lying to you or trying to formulate a lie. These principles can prevent tons of cash and stress also.

CHAPTER 5

SEDUCTION USING VISUAL COMMUNICATION

As social animals, we are the history of using certain non-verbal signals to convey messages appeal to us more so once we are showing interest in others or once we want to converge our interest. Lately, the concept has been complicated since people are taking advantage of the visual communication as a seduction avenue to feed on others. Though there are ancient skills which will be used well to derive incredible results on others. Moreover, it's not limited to attracting the other sex on the same-sex, counting on the orientation or the intention of a private. The most concept of seduction is to urge others' attraction towards you, what you are doing and even towards your perception of how things are done. When one can get the eye of others, they get full attention and control over the connection which makes them be who they're in life.

The power game of seduction is tempting, and it makes men and ladies within the society to pursue their goals regardless of the goals and objective as long as you get what you would like. During this game, only the simplest get control over the opposite. How does one convince, how one conveys the message, and the way it's conceived by the audience is what matters during this concept? As an example, women might want to seduce an upscale guy to urge access to the financial comfort of that guy and the other way around. A singer may tend to seduce the masses through charm and wit to sell his or her music. An official will use all the seduction tactics to urge into that office he desires. All the matters in seduction are the result aided by a well-configured decide to undertake the method of achieving the results.

Basically, seduction is to influence, manipulate or to steer astray to concur the person's mind so as to realize full control over their feelings, perception, and thinking. It are often both negative and positive counting on the motive of the initiator. On the positive end, one can use seduction to deceive people so as to urge something out or abide by their deceits but in an ethical way. On the opposite hand, one can use seduction negatively during a temptation thanks to get people to try to what they might not do under normal circumstances. The deception could also be configured during a threatening thanks to make one accept the offer or manipulative with the incorrect they did within the past that they are doing not want to be revealed to anybody.

How The Body Language Seduction Does Occur?

No got to worry, it are often done practically for better understanding. As an example, drop something on the flow ahead of the category or front of individuals during a gathering, then bend right down to pick. What reaction does one see around you? Does one realize what percentage people have checked out you while picking the staff you had drop that appears in their eyes, how does one perceive it? Generally, people tend to note anybody's movement around them easily. You're likely to urge more attention out of the initial body movement you had created. They're going to turn their heads to watch what you plan to try to next and if you are doing not feed their curiosity immediately, they're likely to urge back to their usual routine. During this way, one can reduce the impact of body movement. Now, what if you are trying something else unique than simply moving or bending down. How they're getting to react to such gestures may surprise you more.

In any case possible, attempt to mirror yourself trying to seduce someone by doing the subsequent, when she crosses her leg, you copy that and do an equivalent. When she raises her head or her hand, copy an equivalent, and whatever she is doing just attempt to do an equivalent.

By copying every move the opposite person makes, it's like forming an interaction with the opposite person. The opposite person tends to select the non-verbal clue from you, and she or he gets interested in what you're doing. The mutual affection created makes both parties like each other, and that they are likely to for a cushy collaboration through mutual affection. During this case, the girl will find you attractive by doing an equivalent body signs or the visual communication match. People could also be getting to such as you thanks to the responsive act they receive. They view you in such how that reflects what they feel inside. Moreover, going to know one another doesn't merely mean knowing their names but also rhyming within the intentions and visual communication which match each other's intention. Though mirroring the intention may sound vague, but taking everything into practice can also make everything possible for both the parties.

Making the intention visible to the prey makes it easy for one to convey the message appropriately. The visual communication interpretation must be seen by the target in q uestion to form it feasible and effective. One must walk on the brink of the person you would like to seduce, take an aim and be within the sector where you'll take a transparent view from others. If that doesn't work well, bump on them more often to make familiarity. People are likely to acknowledge familiar faces than a weird face when it involves seduction tactics. They're going to recognize you instantly when there has been an interaction before the familiar intention. Initially, they'll not recognize your intention, but with consistency, they're likely to acknowledge what you're trying to try to. To maximize the fear, make chitchat about breaking the ice in order that the sensation of being a stranger is minimized. The instant you are doing that, they're likely to open up for the talk, and you never know your lack with the prey in question. If she is that lovely girl you plan to possess, it's the time.

Factually, it's someone who sees you more often; they're likely to become curious about you. That familiarity breeds interest within the other party. We are citizenry, social beings with feelings and sometimes it becomes harder to deny what we feel inside, how we perceive the advance people made on us. Remember, sometimes we long for that one person we could express our feelings to, that one person we will ask without worrying of being judged or discriminated against what you've got done. Sometimes strangers create that avenue that we cannot manage to dodge, all we'd like to try to is to travel with the flow, make that move by accepting their advancement even as to urge that comfort of being wanted, when one tends to urge around you each time, seeking that focus all the time. Who are you to deny or decline the chance to be thereupon one that wants you in their life for once? You never know when such golden opportunity avails next time. Utilize this opportunity as if there's no tomorrow, then sit down and await things to happen your way. Patience pay and if you seek something direly, it's prudent to exercise patience.

Furthermore, one can initiate the art of seduction by creating an accidental touch on the person you plan to seduce. Maybe going to know one another could seem to be difficult at the start, but thereupon magic touch, one will notice of the intention and perhaps realize that you simply have an interest in them.

One can create slightly even while exchanging something or hold a hand for a touch long while greeting the person you're curious about to be you're your friend. This sense of touch will function an ice breaker because the other party is probably going to understand your intention and obtain interested too. Especially, it can suit you well when seducing a lady whom you've got identified as a possible wife or girlfriend. Though this system doesn't apply in every country, only those countries where touching is never wiped out public, or people aren't wont to the act of touching. Therefore, creating the impression within the right place, right timing and with a transparent intention tend to the sport to a topnotch.

Generally, touching may be a quite powerful and effective technique the maximum amount as visual communication cares. Research has revealed that those waitresses who use this system when delivering a bill to customers during a hotel usually get a bigger a part of the tip. More interestingly, customers aren't conscious of this system and the way it's configured to injure their pockets. If they might know that the waitress has nothing to try to with them but money, they might not involve or be vulnerable to the act within the first place. They only get confused with the incorrect impression making them give out a tip inappropriately. The visual communication is at its peak, and therefore the waitress has mastered the art alright that they can't abandoning of it soon. Besides, it's a willing buyer to willing seller though the customer has got to lose his money to prey on the imaginary pleasure, which is conceived in their mind.

In another study on the cashier of a particular store, the salesclerk tends to the touch the hand of the customer while making a transaction or when paying for the merchandise. To customers, it looks like a sort gesture once they are touched by the attendance, and that they are susceptible to frequent the shop to urge such services. On the opposite hand, the cashier who doesn't touch the customer's hand when paying for the merchandise doesn't gain any recognition since there's no impact made on their part. They're just considered like all other shopkeeper who is call at the road to form money. One could also be asking the impact in touching; how does that affect the attitude of an individual whether to shop for from you or not.

Typically, touch is magical, and therefore the body reacts thereto in such how that folks cannot recognize within the first instance. The connectivity created by touch makes one internalize the action in an intimate way that's interpreted within the brain to be a symbol of acceptance. The sensation of being wanted by the one that touches you pleases and makes one feel lively about things. To elaborate a touch more, how will you are feeling to be wanted, needed by the person you're transacting? How is that the feeling of being accepted the way you're appeal to you generally, how will you are feeling if someone is aware of your needs or wants in life? During this situation, the primary cashier seems to worry about the purchasers than the other, which is why may shall transact with him quite the opposite one.

Interestingly, an equivalent concept are often applied during a relationship seduction where the candidate initiates the conversation through slightly. This system is meant to urge the eye of the lady you plan to seduce, and therefore the woman will only get interested if you play your cards throughout the art of touch, which is to trigger their interest. The touch comes with a positive feeling than when it's not done on an individual or towards the prey species.

More often, people will attempt to create an exotic appearance to surprise the suspected prey when seducing. The surprise people get by the way you look tend to tune them towards your way, and it can appear eccentric and exotic to capture the promising adventure in mind. The action of the master of seduction clearly describes this system more elaborately to draw in a memorable ceremony once they first appear within the scene. Such memorable scenes are hard to forget for anyone who is within the gathering. Moreover, this system is generally practiced by the ladies to make a moment impression on the potential husband or boyfriend. Imagine sitting during a bar, and a lady walked during a seductive cloth that reveals a part of their body. The intention of the lady might not be clear to the person at the counter, because the woman might not have configured the intention that somebody is waiting. However, to the person watching at the counter, the visual communication of the lady makes them feel interested in the lady who has just walked into the bar.

As a person who intends to seduce a lady, always attempt to be graceful and assured when walking. Creating a straight back and shoulder taut without bending the backward or forward make one feel confident. Moreover, eye contact plays an important role within the process but should confine mind to make the proper impression through high contact, and stiff eye contact tends to intimidate people and nobody likes such watching all. So take care when making eye contact during the seduction process. It works incredibly, but it also can be your downfall when used wrongly. The key of eye contact when used well, it can land an individual a possible husband or wife. During a study administered by some researchers reveal that seducers are likely to looked at the camera more successfully than the non-seducers. The non-verbal communication skill of eye contact is far impressive and useful in every conversation. Remember that eyes are the window to the soul and when used rightly, one can get a transparent picture of your soul thus creating the attraction.

Most importantly, people that are good at seduction make an excellent countenance to reveal their feelings and intentions well. The positive effect which comes with the countenance is undeniable by the person it's directed to during seduction. If you plan to seduce a lady, get the proper countenance that matches the emotions you're expressing. That expression that divulge to a lady that you simply truly need them and not just out for flattery on them. Nobody are going to be curious about a joker or someone who isn't serious with them. Someone bent joke with their feelings at their pleasure and satisfaction, which doesn't appeal to the opposite party. Most of the time, an honest seducer will apply a trick with the mouth, how they use their mouths, to sum up, the intention to form all things great and possible for the seducer. A sly smile, that brief lips lick expression can make a woman to have an interest in you since she will get the sensation that you simply have an interest in having sex with them or there's something you wish in them, which causes you to lick your lips in such a fashion. However, the key to the present seduction skill is to be subtle and to not overdo the act since some may take it wrongly. Anything overdone usually creates a wrong impression on the target prey, which during this context is that the man or woman you're curious about such a lot.

How can we smell? Does one think that has much to try to with the seduction? Yes, it matters tons, how you'll feel encountering an individual who is smelling sweat everywhere the body. How is that the feeling of interacting with such people within the first place? Besides, how does one feel once you have sweat and close to hug someone within the street. Does one feel confident about yourself or are you only constricted to try to what you've got to do? Naturally, people with an excellent smell in their bodies tend to draw in ladies, and it's the simplest seduction techniq ue for men. Next time you would like to approach that lady you usually admire opposite street, just placed on a pleasing cologne with a pleasing scent that's wont to trigger the condition. Most ladies are tempted to ask the type of perfume you're using, and as a gentleman, you'll take that chance to initiate that talk you dreaded most. That smell of your body is probably going to show them on and make them love you instantly. Who doesn't want to be loved by the other sex unless you're not normal or interested in an eq uivalent sex as your preference?

Ultimately, the tone of the voice are often incorporated within the seduction process, where one is tempted to mix it with countenance, which can make or break the intended bond. In most cases, people may use the proper nonverbal communication skill well until they struggle to speak when the hell breaks loose. How you talk matters tons during the seduction process, which is why it's the last technique to be exercised by any seducer. This system if you are doing not skills to use it well, it can mess you up an enormous deal. Imagine after battling all other techniques, and now your tonal voice is messing you up. How will you are feeling if that happens to you? Most likely you'll not feel good about it in the least, but the funny a part of it's that you simply won't know it until you're done. The person you're lecture won't tell you either, but the reaction or how they turn you off after the entire struggle will show you that your tonal variation wasn't okay. Therefore, making the proper tonal voice is crucial during seduction. Once you make that soft, pleasant tone tend to convey the proper positive emotion to the opposite party successfully. The tone alone is probably going to urge a lady within the right mood to speak to you. Nevertheless, making a harsh and negative tonal voice can create irritation and withdrawal for the opposite party. Using harsh and negative words is probably going to negate the mood created by the non-verbal communication skills during seduction. Sticking to the proper tone all the time matters tons where seduction cares and veered to make a long-lasting relationship.

CHAPTER 6

SELLING YOUR SKILL

One could write the simplest speech on earth, but nobody will probably remember you if you speak during a whisper with a downcast look on your face while delivering that speech. The speech delivery is far important, a bit like the way it should be delivered to the audience. How you speak makes tons of sense quite what you speak. During this case, the speech isn't that important, but the way one delivers that speech is what matters to people. How you utter the scribed words within the speech, the delivery process of your words, how they're being heard by people. It's important to require note of the eyes, crossed arms, and body posture while delivering the message. It matters tons to the audience and also to yourself while selling policy or something you would like people to profit from you. Getting the proper non-verbal communication skill more therefore the visual communication enables one to require advantage of things, take hold and manipulate the audience. The influence is earned by a convincing visual communication that conveys an equivalent message because the body. How it's incorporated to mean an equivalent thing matters tons during this concept.

Strategically, visual communication can help one to stress the argument to form it resonate with the audience, thus attracting their attention and involvement within the whole issue of engagement. If you would like to form your prospective client understand what you plan to sell to them, what you would like them to understand about the merchandise or how you would like them to perceive your undertakings. It's prudent to know the visual communication which appeals to all of them the time, otherwise you ditch getting their attention or making the intended sales. This type of communication may be a crucial a part of communication, which must be taken seriously by the producers, sellers, and intermediaries, more so in business settings. Once you want to drive a crucial home to the audience, consider moving towards them, nodding, maintaining eye contact and smiling make it easier. These gestures create positive air for the audience and also make them feel confident.

For one to spice up the arrogance during the presentation, one must open arms and chest with a stiff straight back. The position makes one breathe well while delivering the speech to the audience. Making the simplest presentation enables one to make an honest rapport with the audience. That rapport created can end up to be friendship for several people, which helps them in succeeding in business sales. Remember that only sales challenges can help the business to make a competitive advantage within the market.

When it involves sales, attitude determines the overall outcome of the negotiation, whet we put into the conversation highly depends on our attitude. Challenges are everywhere, and other people should learn to surpass the consequential conversations, which tend to interrupt our tendency to win the conversation — having that in mind, we will create an honest impression through visual communication and therefore the general outward appearance for the task. Having an equivalent boring business call over and over doesn't change anything, it's the keenness we put into our tone attitude which will turn tables not our favor, how we would like things to be and therefore the goals and objectives set to be fulfilled.

Engaging eyes, as against dull gaze, can win someone over to your way of thinking, it can help an individual to specialize in the intended message. If you look someone within the eye while talking, they feel that you simply have an interest in what's being said, and you're vouching into their ideas. Nevertheless, one should take care to not overdo that because it'd mean that you simply are staring oddly during a creepy way which will not appeal to people. Moreover, one should attempt to smile while speaking, and therefore the smile relaxes muscles on your face making it admirable. It further creates a welcoming expression that permits the opposite party to feel appreciated and adored within the quite relationship you're both having at that point. However, take care to not overdo the smile since one can easily detect a deceiving smile alright thus making the conversation to be dull and unamusing. Also, when making a purchase, you ought to always make sure that you think about the behavior of the opposite party who is out there for chase and check out to convince them in such how that they're made aware that you simply can do the task.

Most of the time, making a purchase are often a desperate business which will leave you chewing your nails, tearing your hair out, biting your lips, and making other miserable gestures. On the opposite hand, it are often good rolling fun once you have mastered all its flows and bliss to its parry to the commercial world. It all depends on how one perceives doing deals or going after every deal that needs their commitment, perseverance, and wit of connecting with others. Without connection, one cannot achieve personal selling and business might not be your thing at the top of the day. Not forgetting that folks only need those that make them feel important, wanted and adore in society. If you can't create that sense of importance, adoration and need in business dealing or during personal selling, you're doom to fail. Who on earth doesn't want to be appreciated, wanted and adored by others? Even the politicians always adore the psychopaths who keep it up praising them wherever they are going, those that praise them highly and make names for them are those appreciated by these people. Then how on earth will you plan to win that sales talk if you are doing not consider your client to be worthy, great in potential to suit your needs. That's very scary, but it's the reality that folks should remember of, accept and adopt so as to achieve any dealing.

However, when selling, one should strive to seem at the speaker while sharing a thought. This shows that you simply are at an equivalent level and are conscious of what they're browsing, how they feel, how they capture the entire idea to form it worth sharing, and the way they typically view other things from their perspective. Moreover, one should make certain to stay the gaze open and appealing to the speaker in order that it doesn't attract the other negative feelings. In other words, an open gaze creates how for the speaker to know your concern about the matter also. Just in case you're allowed to precise your concern, make certain to reflect on the speech of the previous speaker to form them appreciated, adored and well understood.

But beat all, the visual communication expression during that speech is what determines the extent of understanding, comprehension of the ideas and therefore the general perceptions of these ideas. In any case possible, one should nod while the opposite person is speaking. It creates a positive feeling on the speaker, and that they desire that they had won the battle even before making the purpose clear to everyone. That nodding makes the impression that you simply are empathetic, appreciative and curious about what one is saying, and you're willing to choose their ideas for greatness.

Leaning forward when someone is speaking can create an honest gesture that you simply don't want to invade their territory. The act of moving on the brink of the person speaking otherwise you shall have a conversation with shows that you simply have an interest in them and prepared to concentrate. It doesn't matter the type of conversation you plan to possess with them. What matters is that the way you express yourself to them, how ready you're to urge their full attention while speaking. This type of gesture can win you a client when during a business setting where the attentiveness is very considered a sort of respect. It are often aided with an open hand gesture when engaging during a vibrant conversation that needs much attention. When doing so, the opposite party should notice that you simply are just doing it unconsciously and not forcing it to happen. The keenness which comes with such gestures should represent itself, and therefore the realization of its impact are going to be felt when the opposite person reacts during a reciprocating way.

If you would like to form a transparent visual communication when making a purchase, one should strive to mirror their accent in such how that it appeals to the audience — ensuring that you simply speak at an equivalent speed with the admirable tone, which doesn't contradict the overall visual communication. That feelings and perceptions should match the speech for it to be effective to the audience and therefore the general public consumption. In most cases, you'll be required to form a speech to an outsized audience, and when such times come, be prepared to take advantage of the chance to figure on your favor. By doing so, you'll be ready to attract more positivity towards your way, and therefore the general perception actualized accordingly. Therefore, mirroring such events before they occur enables one to possess a conceivable future direction and desire towards achieving the set objectives. It's like having a concrete plan configured towards achieving the set goals and objectives in business or life generally. That strategic plan enables one to make a competitive advantage within the market. During this case, the market is that the desired objective the opposite competitors are aiming at a bit like you. In every conversation, there's an intention, and for everything to figure your way, you want to have clear set goals and making them clear to the opposite party need a convincing accent. Just in case you are feeling too fast, it can create an impact that you simply are putting more pressure on the opposite person. While once you speak too slowly, it can indicate that you simply are too lazy or unconcerned about the matter in hand. Mirroring this before delivering the speech causes you to practice well and enable you to perceive the likely outcome of your speech delivery.

Interestingly, remaining calm when someone is making a speech can provides a positive impression on the speaker. They're going to think that you simply are attentive and in agreement with what they're saying. In other words, it makes one feel positively attached to what they're saying, and therefore the knowledge that there's a caring listener within the crowd makes them feel awesome. Ever wonder why some people feel good once you shut one's mouth once they are talking? Why they like that nodding quite replies and questions triggered towards them while speaking. It's very interesting how it works wonders on people, and therefore the same are often applied when talking or selling policy to the opposite party. Once you allow them to talk, express their feelings, worries, and emotions whether negative or positive. The art of listening makes them feel welcomed, wanted, appreciated and valued by the listener. Albeit you're selling a bar of gold during which everybody knows its value and importance at a lower cost, master the art of listening in an efficient way that elicits the emotions of the speaker. By doing so, you're likely to win them, win their trust and their friendship, which can end in a long-lasting relationship. In business, all you would like is connectivity forged through friendship and not a customer who will buy from you today and go forever. One should take care when making such engagement. It's going to mean smaller to you, but it means much to the opposite person.

Ultimately, one should take caution on how they greet, be it during a meeting, casual gathering, or high places. All that matters are how you perform yourself when making that crucial handshake. The pressure put into it matters tons and don't mistake handshake intended for ladies to appeal for men. It doesn't work that way; women prefer a mild and caring handshake while men need that hand and pressured handshake to work out the arrogance during a person. Therefore, when shaking hands with men, make certain to try to it well; it can either sell you out or make things worse.

CHAPTER 7

NEGOTIATION WITH SIMPLE MOVES

Successful negotiation entails many things, and it's little to try to with just saying the proper thing. It's been proven that commanding visual communication plays an important role when negotiating more so when it's during a business setting. Mastering this essential skill can pivot one to the very best income generating dealing ever. However, it's little to try to with what you learn in school or taught in psychology schools. It's a practical phenomenon that has got to be practiced and enhanced with time. What matters most is that the skill of mastery you set into it. Foremost, one must mirror the opposite person's actions, visual communication, and general behavior as portrayed when one is talking. Through that, one can easily understand the vocal tone and therefore the countenance of the speaking enabling them to create the rapport necessary for the negotiation. As an example, when an opportunity is talking on stage, leaning forward and following the conversation, make one connect quickly with the speaker. The speaker will notice the interest and therefore the positive influence you've got within the speech.

Moreover, it's the interest that matters most during this instance where the speaker and therefore the listener can connect on a mutual ground of interest. Later you'll connect well since negotiation rapport had been created during the speech delivery. In case, you recline and cross your arms during that speech delivery; the speaker may wonder if you're curious about their choice of a subject or there's something wrong. When this happens, make certain that the negotiation has begun on a negative point of view and perhaps you'll not win in such a case. Nobody likes a challenge, and when it involves negotiation, you would like to challenge your partner in such a positive way. Furthermore, nodding negotiation skills are often adopted from the previous president of the US, barrack Obama; from all his speeches, you'll easily notice this unique negotiation skill in action. The president adopted this system even when, in total disagreement with the delegates, he will always nod and keep eye contact in the least times. They clearly are often traced back to his dramatic win during the election when he was delivering his speech. If you'll recall, he's the foremost eloquent and presentable guy thus far. How he delivers his speech, how he talks, and therefore the quite negotiation he employs in his career is irreplaceable. No wonder he achieved tons during his tenure.

Moreover, negotiation skills can help in defusing tension within the mass and build endless alignment towards achieving an objective. It also helps to create bridges between the whites and therefore the blacks within the country. Besides, the negotiation skill employed by the highest state official enables the country to realize power through the treaties signed by these people to assist the state get to its level. How will you convince an individual if you can't convince yourself? Does it make any sense at all? The skill is mandatory for any business one that desires to urge on top of the sport. It compels patience and a deep understanding of the flows involved within the system.

Additionally, one should concentrate to the hands, how they're getting used to convey a message. Stress and nervousness are always shown in by the hand movement. During this instance, it becomes very hard to cover the emotions since one can catch on during the hands. How you fidget your hands while talking and the way your things are portrayed by the utilization of the hand can tell how a problem is serious, otherwise you are just joking with people. Moreover, an understanding or adviser will always see it through the way you employ the hands. When hands are clasp together tightly while communicating, it can depict that you simply are nervous and scared of something. An honest negotiator will always cash in of such situations to urge what they need from you and even get the higher a part of your attention. At this level, all it means is that you simply are susceptible to any attack which will be triggered your way by anyone. Defending yourself becomes very difficult when signs of vulnerability and mediocrity are observed. These are signs of weakness, and anyone can easily fall for such setbacks, but showing it publicly is what can drain the entire relationship. To counter such tragic events, one should learn to place hands below the chest and grasp the fingers together ahead of you to fain confidence while talking. When it's done rightly, one can get all it takes from the audience and therefore the observer. What does one need if it's not the influence while talking, the manipulation that comes with it, and the way to sway people into your way of thinking. An excellent negotiator always knows the way to persuade people to their way of thinking, perception, point of view and therefore the beliefs of their act. Getting that influence to need a skill that inbuilt skill that can't be repudiated by anyone in society. One should have a longlasting impact on the partner for them to be approved by things of the society at large. An important person always knows the way to use his or her hand when talking or when communicating with others publicly.

Similarly, how you plant your feet during negotiation represent itself. It can either sell you out or cause you to drain into your pit. Though it's little to try to with the negotiation, one can easily depict from your feet, if it's firmly planted into the bottom or when it's dwindling on top of the opposite while sitting or standing. The message are often perceived rightly when your foot is unsettled to point out that you simply are nervous or not comfortable with things. One can easily tell once you are lying or telling the reality by watching your feet.

Correspondingly, non-verbal behavior plays an excellent role during negotiation. These behaviors radiate back to openness, confidence, and honesty which copy the optimistic behavior seen in most of the high performers. By employing the proper negotiation skill, they will reach a mutually satisfying agreement at the top of everything. How people do behave can indicate their true state of mind, how they perceive things and therefore the way they act on every activity. By reading their true attitude and intentions, one can get a full view of their way of life, and negotiation becomes very easy.

It is prudent to find out much about the person you're close to negotiate within time before any plan to make any move. Knowing their culture, beliefs, and therefore the perception they need towards the topic help in alleviating the success of the negotiation. One must show up in time on the day they're to barter on any subject. It helps in getting the negotiation on the proper foot, and it shows that you simply value time and every one which is there to form on-time without wastage by dwindling around trying to dodge during a different way. How does one feel once you are the primary person to reach the venue or arriving at the designated time as scheduled? Be careful before you open your mouth during negotiation, how are the reactions around you, how do they view you generally to urge it done or how do they welcome you to the venue. Take care about every action within the room before you discuss anything; it can prevent an excellent deal. It's not your business to discuss anything you see, hear or perceived once you go somewhere new unless they seek your view thereon. Back to your arrival, being late is perceive to be disrespectful and discourteous. Generally, it's insulting to be late to your first meeting. It shows that you simply can't be trusted or being ordained to high positions by anyone who cares for his or her time. In short, you're incompetent, and integrity is questionable by the opposite party. How will you retain on lying about your reason for being late albeit they accept the apology otherwise you want them to urge wont to it in order that once they agree on the negotiation terms there'll not be any problem? It doesn't work that way, and albeit it's so, it'll become very hard at the top of it all.

Interestingly, one can easily identify the baseline behavior before stepping into any negotiation. There's an important chance of meeting the prospects and have a coupon chat before stepping into serious business. At now is when one can easily establish the type of behavior, they're likely to encounter during negotiation. During normal charting with strangers, they're real, and their behavior are often seen within the way they talk, reason, and consider things on different subjects. If you would like to urge the negotiation to favor you, observe use of these times once you can easily talk with none pressure involved unlike when during a meeting setting. Pre- negotiation usually determines how one will likely behave when faced with pressure during the important negotiation. One can easily predict their turning point, what tune them to behave during a certain way, what irritates them, and what amuse them. By observing these factors well, you'll escape on the way to affect them while negotiating for business purpose or when there's an important deal you would like them to involve you certain own benefit. How they react when answering questions during prenegotiations chat can determine their honesty or witty way of getting things done. If there's a relaxed, composed countenance when answering an issue, you'll conclude that they're honest and may be trusted. Just in case they're not honest, you'll notice give-away behavior amid shuffling of feet, tense facial expressions, and other awkward excuses once they don't skills to convince you to their way of thinking. It'll be very difficult to take care of such a conversation since there'll be no flow of events. Constructing one lie after the opposite usually becomes very difficult, and in most cases, they're going to attempt to avoid the topic. In such a case, know that you simply are being duped into shit, which you can't remove yourself. Therefore, when engaging in real conversation during the negotiation, don't forget the previous behavior. Attempt to observe if they're repeated within the negotiation process. Just in case you sense any of it, attempt to line up of yourself and don't continue in such negotiation since there are high chances that you simply are being played.

Alternatively, one should get notice of the countenance when negotiating with a client, partner, or business associate. Observe the breathing pattern, eyes, mouth movement, and jaw of those people. These features can predict their thoughts, emotions, and intentions for the negotiation. One should note that even the temperature of an individual can tell much about the person's psychological state. Knowing to watch different facial expressions sign can help one to save lots of much of the investment, which can be a results of cheating, fraudulent behaviors, and scum, which are done unnoticed. As an example, frowning and tense lips can show that somebody doesn't accept as true with your point of view and it indicates that you simply should change your way of thinking or how you are doing things.

Ultimately, there's how that one can twist their mouth to depict that they are doing not such as you, or they are doing not approve your intended action. By observing these signs, one can make the proper decision before things turn worse. You ought to know that negative behavior displayed during negotiation clearly shows how close-minded an individual is, how recalcitrance and disinterested within the subject. In response to such negative gestures, one can nod in agreement, lean towards the client with a controlled calm face to point out respect for his or her decision and perception of the event. By doing so, they're going to not detect that you simply have unraveled their deceit.

Chapter 8: Public Speaking Body Language

Body language are often defined because the non-verbal cues that somebody uses while making a speech. Visual communication is a crucial aspect that each orator should have. These nonverbal cues from the bottom foundation for your speech both before you begin and even after starting your speech. They're going to give impact to the message you're passing, how it's being received and the way they appear at you as their speaker. A speaker could have the simplest speech ever prepared but how they deliver it's all that matters. Having the ability to figure on your visual communication can make an enormous difference in how you relate to your audience. This is often always the primary step publicly speaking before having the ability to know your audience's visual communication also. Recognizing the visual communication of an audience can tell you tons about what the audience feels about you, how they're receiving your message. For instance, an audience may start whispering while you're the middle of your speech because you're not audible and clear enough. A speaker who isn't ready to tell why their audiences are whispering will have failed at their job and therefore the audience won't have gotten the message that you simply wanted to pass. An honest speaker should behave the acceptable visual communication while lecture their audience and even be ready to understand the audience's visual communication also. It's important to know that visual communication can cause you to succeed or fail. Observing the proper visual communication, which is for you and your audience, you'll be ready to succeed while you fail if you can't observe your visual communication. Tons of individuals practice on speech alone but forget on the important part which is body behavior. A speaker who has gained the power to read and control their visual communication doesn't have a tough time trying to work out what their audience is saying. An honest speaker should be ready to influence the audience into doing and understanding what they're saying. They're uninfluential within the society and that they often are used as public figures when it involves public meetings and public gatherings. They will easily settle down an angry crowd and ask them get their grievances and also show them the answer of their situations and problems. However, learning the way to use your visual communication which of others takes time to find out and energy. An honest speaker can make an impression on their audience such everybody taking note of them would walk out having a special idea of what they thought. They ought to be ready to bring out multiple channels of communication between them and their audience. The subsequent are visual communication that each good speaker should have.

Power pose

Having a strong pose makes one feel powerful and contributes to an increase in testosterone levels thereby increasing your dominance. This pose makes the audience such as you as they begin admiring your dominance. This is often done by, standing straight together with your shoulders back and your legs width apart, rest your shoulders centrally and check out to focus, place your hand on either side of your body which can assist you make gestures easily if need be and lastly face your audience at the most of your speech. Always walk round the room to form sure that each audience within the room features a clear view of you and is confident about you.

Eye contact

Making and maintaining eye contact together with your audience creates a connection between you and this makes the audience feel loved and valued. They will respect you and hear you because you've got made them feel important. The audience can trust you and whatever you're saying, this is often because it's known that folks don't make eye contact once they are lying. Making eye contact is additionally the simplest way during which you'll get honest feedback from your audience. You'll tell whether your audience is listening, bored, curious about your topic, tired, happy then many other things. Happening together with your |along with your"> together with your speech without making any eye contact with your audience could make them angry. It's ethically said that when lecture an outsized number of individuals you ought to maintain eye contact with one member within the audience for a minimum of four or more seconds before moving to the opposite member. Use the zigzag notioon while making eye contact together with your audience, that is, check out one member at the rear left, then back right, then to the front left and front right. While at this you ought to confirm that you simply do that with different members of the audience. This may assist you connect with as many of the members as possible. If during a case of 1 on one setting, maintain eye contact with the person for ten seconds then provides it an opportunity. This could even be applied when during a question and answer scenario.

Hand gestures

Using the right hand gestures also can help enhance your message even further. This also causes you to feel confident and more relaxed because they assist you amplify your speech and make it believable. This is often an important a part of visual communication that helps people understand what you're feeling. For instance, putting your verbs into action like showing the action of playing football are often brought out by the utilization of your hands. On how important the utilization of gestures are often it's also good to form sure that you simply don't overuse it this is able to cause you to look nervous before the audience or as if you're unsure of what you're saying. Gestures are more defined and stronger so it's good that you simply don't overuse them. Use gestures to speak numbers and position and descriptive gestures to point out movement, for instance, length. You'll use emotional gestures like clapping your hands to point out a plea. Use can use different body parts for your gestures just like the feet and arm.

Movement

Moving around shows the audience that you simply are confident and you've got the facts straight for whatever you're saying. Movement helps you include your audience in your conversation. Your audience are going to be more engaged and can be ready to trust your message since you've got already proved to be confident. While making your movements confirm that you simply don't pace round the stage every thirty seconds this may distract your audience. Take time after one move to require the opposite one. Skills to form the transition of your topics as you go from one topic to a different. During the question and answer time, it's good that you simply move towards the audience and have interaction them from there. This may assist you grasp the eye of your listeners.

Expression

These are mostly facial expressions that a speaker might use to stress their point. The audience can interpret your feelings and thoughts by just watching your facial expressions. It's important to understand that the faces you create should interconnect with what you're talking about. For instance, you can't laugh

158

while giving out a speech at a funeral, it might sound awkward and bizarre. These countenance s ted to confuse people as you would possibly find the opposite person interprets your facial expression during a way that you simply don't. For instance, a frowned face shows that somebody is angry, while others might interpret it as confusion, so your countenance should be clear to everyone.

Mannerisms

These are habits that the majority people do this they do not feel anything wrong about them but the opposite party feels very uncomfortable and feels very offended. These behaviors might include placing your hands within the pocket, twiddling with your hands, using words like 'um'. Sort of a good speaker, you ought to be ready to know and understand that you simply have these habits and it's hard for you to prevent. After acknowledgment work towards fighting them off since they're irritating. Facing your audience after you've got cleared these habits will make your audience more involved in your discussions.

Breathing

Breathing is additionally a crucial think about speechmaking especially once you are feeling nervous. Maintaining a slow breath will assist you calm down and forego the nervousness. Relaxed breathes also make sure that you're talking during a relaxed state and pace. Breathing heavily or fast can increase your nervousness and also you can't be heard properly due to the fast-talking and breathing. Performing some breathing exercises before starting your speech is extremely important. Ensuring that you simply get up straight and you are doing not fight for breath is additionally a crucial visual communication. An honest speaker with the motive to influence their audience should be ready to control their breathing and nervousness ahead of their audiences taking note of them.

Voice

Your vocal expression tells tons about you and therefore the speech you're almost to deliver. The audience are going to be ready to remember a speaker who was loud and had confidence in his voice.

A speaker must convince the audience that they know that they're talking about. This may influence the audience ethically because the speaker can know each side of the arguments and may present it correctly. Understanding your audience are going to be an honest factor which will help a speaker be ready to influence their audiences. Having the character of your audiences at the rear of your mind will assist you know and research more on the topic matter and check out to repair it during a way that matches your audience's approach of reasoning and way of viewing things. Having the ability to cite relevant quotes and citations in your speech will capture the eye of your audiences and during this state, it's easy to control them and have them reason alongside you. It's good that you simply make references especially for things that you feel need more references. After the speaker now has all this ready and may understand their feelings, they will now be ready to learn more about their audiences. A speaker would be ready to know when the audience is listening or when the audience doesn't seem to overcome together with your speech. Public speakers can easily influence and manipulate people in society.

The ultimate goal for speechmaking has got to gain members' attention but it's not a simple task all an equivalent. Public speakers are known to be the pillar of society. Having special and simply body languages assist you listening to your speech. An honest speaker for any kind can change the bad habits of a student who had fallen into addiction. This is often because, at now, they will distinguish different body languages and expressions that the audiences use as you continue together with your speech. An honest speaker should have the arrogance to control people ethically and help them forego their bad habits. The visual communication as explained above relates to both the speaker and therefore the audience role within the speech. It's also good to notice that while preparing for a speech, the speaker must first consider the moral conditions of speechmaking, learn and understand their audience. A speaker that sets out their minds to assist people in their speech will always re-evaluate their speech once again and if possible, act an equivalent speech to your friends and allow them to tell you if your presentation is okay. Being persuasive and influential to people helps people gain tons of trust in you and that they tend to believe whatever you tell them. Such public speakers with such ethical grounds are capable of adjusting the ideas of an entire community only through several words and talks. It's however been proven that an honest orator one who is influential requires to find out visual communication to up their game publicly speaking.

Conclusion

Thank you for creating it through to the top of book title, let's hope it had been informative and ready to provide you with all of the tools you would like to realize your goals whatever they'll be.

The next step is to urge to action and apply what you've got learned from the book. Note that, learning the way to analyze people may be a wide topic that doesn't stop here. Therefore, it's beneficial for you to continue learning and find other equally beneficial resources where you'll get the knowledge you seek regarding the way to analyze people. From the chapters you understand that analyzing people doesn't need to be for unethical reasons, it's also possible to research people and use the knowledge you gather ethically. As an example, you'll analyze a client during a negotiation to understand whether or not they are serious clients or not and also, to know their references within the sales negotiation.

The bottom line is that we should always not analyze people for unethical reasons. We should always specialize in using the knowledge we gather from analyzing people to raised react to their message and actions. It causes you to seem smart and more at sync with people once you are ready to react to their actions without overreacting just because you understand what they really wish to convey whether their words convey it effectively or not.

This book was designed to assist you find out how to research people for a far better environment and better relations with people. As an example, by understanding the various personality types, you're better ready to comprehend and work with people that have different personalities without making anyone feel unwanted or not understood in every situation. As such, it's important for managers and leaders to find out the way to analyze people for the straightforward reason that they manage people with different personalities and that they must make sure that everyone remains motivated to figure and be productive.

Therefore, after gathering the much and beneficial information from this book, it's important for you to also teach the people around you ways to research the people they work and relate with on a day to day. This is often ethical in that; it helps people react to issues better also as relationships with the people around them better. We all want to measure in an accommodative world and that we should be willing to try to what it takes to realize that. This includes helping people around us analyze other people's actions and reacting to them accordingly without hurting their feelings.

If at now you're still wondering why you ought to invest overtime to know the way to analyze people, you'll be avoiding the importance of identifying gestures, postures, and expressions that assist you to be a far better person also. Moreover, if you would like to speak your feelings without talking much or speaking, understanding the various body languages is that the thanks to go. This is often what most of the people apply once they refuse to speak to their partners and apply what they call "cold war". They let their actions and visual communication do the speaking and communicate what they really feel. Within the end, the partner understands that they're not happy about something and that they either ask the way to change things or better still do what's required of them. This is often the right example of how an individual can apply visual communication and the way people can read visual communication during a bid to save lots of a situation.

Finally, if you found this book useful in any way, a review on amazon is usually appreciated!